THE INCREDIBLE LIFE OF A HIMALAYAN YOGI

THE INCREDIBLE LIFE OF A HIMALAYAN YOGI

Shuddhaanandaa Brahmachari

The Incredible Life of a Himalayan Yogi

Published by Lokenath Divine Life Mission, Kolkata

5th Reprint June 2016

Edited by Ann Shannon

For more information about Baba Lokenath:
www.babalokenath.org

Lokenath Divine Life Mission
277 Shantipally, Kasba
Kolkata - 700 107, India
ldlmcal@gmail.com

Lokenath Divine Life Fellowship, USA
susan@feelinghearts.org

For all who read the book it would be a great pleasure to have your comments and feelings about the Book or about the great Sage Baba Lokenath. Please write to susan@feelinghearts.org and we will personally answer your mail.

ISBN: 8187207078
ISBN 13: 9788187207078

DEDICATION

To

My beloved father and mother, my first spiritual teachers whose blessings and love paved the way to the world of Light and Love and the grace of the Great Masters.

CONTENTS

Baba Lokenath's Cottage, Baradi (Bangladesh)

Shuddhaanandaa Brahmachari

PREFACE

AUTHOR'S VISION OF BABA LOKENATH

THE DIVINE GRACE descends when the time ripens. I was in the monastery in the initial days of my monastic life in the suburbs of Calcutta; of course going through the phase of discovering a new life that dwells in the depth of our own superficiality. Then the golden moment came, on 15 October 1978, the great Himalayan Master Baba Lokenath Brahmachari (1730-1890) appeared in a vision and revealed to me the purpose of my being in the path of Light and the task ahead. I asked him many questions that were bothering me, and he answered them all with infinite love and compassion. Then he asked me "Why have you stopped writing?" I was a bit taken aback, how could he know that I used to keep journal of my revered Master's conversations, which I had stopped. He continued, " I read your writes, I liked them," then he just lifted his long right hand into the air and waved it in a circular motion and said "Write and spread out".

Years later I left the ashram and as a wandering mendicant in Himalayas reached a place called Bageshwar, famous for holy confluence and an ancient Shiva Temple. There, on the top of a mountain, I built a small retreat with a temple of Baba Lokenath and started my practice of deeper contemplation. The inspiration to write the first ever English Biography of Baba Lokenath came at this time. It was an experience to write the life and teachings of Mahayogi, just being a humble instrument allowing the Divine writer to flow through me. It was not just writing a book or biography by collecting information and putting them chronologically, but to me it was my penance, my spiritual practice. For in the course of writing this book, by the grace of the Master, I could visualize the episodes and times of Baba Lokenath, and just translate those visions into words that flowed without much effort. When the ascended Masters ordain anyone to do a divine task, then it is the power of the Master that completes the task. Yes, that has been my deepest experience; I could feel my instrumentation and how silently it also brought about an inner transformation for which I have been longing and meditating for years.

As you read this book, please know that very little is known about Baba Lokenath's long life of 160 years, for he was against any propaganda about him or his incomprehensible powers of manifesting miracles. But this book has his presence, for it is his divine grace that made this book possible. Whoever will read this book will feel the aura of his divine presence surrounding. It is no coincidence that you have this book and you are reading the life of one who could say, "In danger, remember me, I will save you." I tell you, he keeps his promise, and you can try.

Please read his promises, his teachings and the lives of those who came in touch with him and the transformations they attained, particularly, his equanimity, his infinite love for animals and his boundless compassion for mankind.

May you be blessed with peace and joy in your life, and feel the presence of the Master removing all the obstacles from the path of life to your ultimate journey of retreating back Home.

Shuddhaanandaa Brahmachari

CHAPTER 1

BABA LOKENATH: TOTAL DIVINITY IN HUMAN FORM

Om Ganeshaya Namaha
Om Namo Bhagavate Sri Lokenathaya

THE PROMISE

"Whenever you are in danger, whether in war, forest, ocean or jungle, remember Me. I shall save you.

"You may not know me. You may not realize who I am. Just pray to me with a little touch of your heart, and I shall free you from gripping sorrows and miseries.

"I willingly reveal myself to you so that you can reach me. Otherwise it would be impossible.

"No power on heaven or earth can damage the devotees who take shelter under me, for there is no one greater than I who can touch you.

"I can do whatever I like. It is only your lack of trust, your non-belief that keeps your desires unfulfilled.

"For those who with love and devotion surrender to me, if they are in trouble, my heart melts. This is my compassion. And with my compassion, my power flows out to them, freeing them from miseries and unhappiness.

"I am Eternal. I am Deathless. I AM."

WHO IS BABA LOKENATH?

THESE ASTOUNDING WORDS of assurance to suffering humanity were spoken by one of the greatest yogis ever born, Brahmarishi Baba Lokenath Brahmachari, who lived from 1730-1890. Who is Baba Lokenath that he would dare to make such a promise, a promise akin to that of Lord Krishna when speaking to Arjuna on the battlefield of Kurukshetra:

> "Surrender to Me alone. I shall deliver you of all sins. My devotees never perish."
> (Bhagavad Gita 18/66)

How could Baba Lokenath make a promise akin to Jesus' promises in the New Testament?

> "Ask, and you will receive. Seek and you will find. Knock, and the door will be opened to you." (Mathew 7: 7-8)

> "Whatever you ask in My name, it will be given unto you."
> (John 14:14)

There is nothing more powerful than the promise of an enlightened being. The enlightened don't lie, ever. And they don't make or take such promises lightly. But Baba's promises go far beyond those of most enlightened beings. In the breadth and scope of his pledge to us, he reveals a level of divine mastery which is rare, even among the enlightened.

While it is impossible for us to comprehend the magnitude of realization prompting a promise of this order, it does behoove us to draw near, with an open and expectant heart, to the One who promises. Baba Lokenath calls us to him, reaching across the distance of a century, eager to uplift every dimension of our lives. He reaches out with an intensity of love and compassion, extended as the active and intervening hand of grace, to heal our ills and personal deficiencies, however large or small, however tenacious they may seem, however hopeless we feel about them.

And however much the promise fulfilled may uplift the circumstances of our lives, inner and outer, its true and ultimate benefit lies in the stream of Divine Life which the promise brings us closer to.

BABA'S LIFE, PRACTICE AND ATTAINMENT

Baba Lokenath attained a state of divinity which is beyond all human comprehension. Most yogis focus on a particular yogic path, that of Jnana (path of discriminating knowledge), Karma (path of selfless action), Bhakti (path of devotional surrender to the Divine), or Ashtanga (Patanjali's) Yoga to lead them to Ultimate Reality. Baba, however, diligently practiced the principles of all four. Sri Chaitanya

Mahaprabhu, the Divine Incarnation of Bhakti, taught the world the path of Bhakti alone. Jagadguru Sankaracharya taught only the path of Jnana. Baba Lokenath is the Divine Incarnation of Jnana, Karma, Bhakti and Ashtanga Yoga. Mastering all of them, Baba became the Incarnation of their synthesis, the living essence and full embodiment of the universal religion of love, the *Sanatana Dharma*, which is taught in the *Bhagavad Gita*. Baba taught, from the essence of his exalted being, that the *Bhagavad Gita* is more than scripture. It is an eternal song meant to be sung through the medium of our lives. As the living example of his own teaching, Baba came to be called "The Song of the Living Gita."

Baba's mastery was at every level of being and form. He attained total Divinity in human form, which his name, Lokenath (master of the worlds) denotes. Baba Lokenath realized Ultimate Perfection on the physical plane, the divinization of human form, which is the final and most difficult transformation, through an extraordinarily prolonged period of sadhana. Playing the role of the perfect disciple, humbly and completely surrendered to the Lotus Feet of his beloved Guru through eighty years of intensive austerities in both the jungles of the lower plains and snow-covered regions of the Himalayas, Baba was granted enlightenment of the highest order. Lokenath was ninety years old. His Gurudev was a grand old man of 150 years.

The enlightened Lokenath soon discovered that he had surpassed his beloved Guru. Guru Bhagwan Ganguly had selflessly led Lokenath to that exalted state before personally attaining Liberation. Surprised, stricken with sadness, and filled with compassion, Lokenath wept for his Master.

Understanding Lokenath's tears, Guru Bhagwan smiled tenderly and reassured his disciple there was only cause for joy. He knew he would soon shed his old body and quickly return to Lokenath in his next incarnation. He asked Lokenath to then lead him to his enlightenment through the path of integral yoga. Upon hearing Guru Bhagwan's plan, Lokenath, overwhelmed with gratitude, promised to grant his wish. Weeping with joy, Lokenath prostrated himself at his Master's feet.

Baba Lokenath's relationship with Guru Bhagwan is unique in its tenderness. It is rare, if not unprecedented, for the disciple to accept responsibility for leading the master to realization of Ultimate Reality. The reversal of Guru and disciple roles, with the newly enlightened disciple immediately prostrating himself at the unenlightened Guru's feet, and the Guru requesting his disciple to lead him to enlightenment, is an exquisite and touching revelation of mutual, mirrored humility. It serves to remind us of the true selflessness of all genuine spiritual attainment, as well as of the endless, delicate and unpredictable beauty of divine unfoldment.

Empowered with total Divinity, Baba Lokenath boldly proclaimed a father's boundless love to his children of coming generations:

"For more than a hundred years, I have traveled through the hills and mountains and have amassed enough spiritual treasures. You shall sit at home and enjoy the fruits of my austerities."

He had achieved the highest that could be achieved in the human form. From the total transformation of his gross body to his subtlest being, he left no path untouched, and flowered into the embodiment of Purna Avatar— God Himself.

As the living embodiment of integral yoga, Baba manifested the ultimate human potential, attaining Oneness with the Divine at every level. Showing the path of discriminating knowledge, devotion, and Karma Yoga, Baba demonstrated movement in the world of dynamic activity, with the heart committed to the Divine, and with the intelligence in alliance with the ground of the pure Cosmic Potentiality and Cosmic Intelligence.

Baba taught, *"Knowledge of the Self is the only way to liberation. Devotion is the essence. Mantra, etc., are the supportive aspects. Move along the path with devotion and love, and who can obstruct your way? You are all my children!"*

Baba stressed devotion to and love for one's own Guru and to the Divine. Knowledge of the Self, however, is equally important. Baba emphasized critical vigilance of one's own mind. Through continual self-assessment, with the grace of the guru, one is brought to innate, pure intelligence, which is connected to the subtle nature of cosmic design. Intuitive perception of subtle truths blooms with steady self-examination, lovingly offered at the feet of the guru with the prayer for purification.

Rather than outward renunciation, which can become an escape, Baba asks for action performed with the spirit of service to the Divine. Whoever seeks Baba's grace is guided, often in inscrutable ways, to inner transformation, without the necessity for drastic changes in normal social and family life.

THE TALE OF THE KUMBHAMELA

The following story conveys the rarity of a teacher of Baba's stature, even among the enlightened, coming to live in the world.

Kumbhamela, one of the greatest festivals of the Hindus, is held once every twelve years. Millions of Hindus from all over the world congregate at the bank of the holy river where the festival is held, with the location occurring on a rotating basis. On this year, it was to be held at Prayag, which is in Allahabad, close to Varanasi. It was the Purna Kumbha, which is deemed the most holy and auspicious time for bathing at the holy confluence of the Ganges and Yamuna Rivers. Prayag became the holiest confluence not only due to the assembly of thousands of sadhus and sannyasins, but above all, because of the great numbers of Himalayan sages and yogis who have come down to the planes for this Kumbhamela for thousands of years.

A devotee of Baba Lokenath was visiting this holy fair. With a picture of Baba in his pocket, he felt that Baba was with him. With Baba's grace, the devotee felt confident he would see and meet great living saints of the time. Baba had once said to him,

"My child, never miss an opportunity to meet the realized saints, for their blessings and presence will inspire deeper devotion and love for the Divine and Guru. Satsang, being in the company of the holy ones, who live the Truth, is the greatest blessing of the Lord."

That year, the greatest attraction of the festival was a very old sage from the Himalayas who not only possessed incredible mystical powers, but whose love and compassion for suffering souls was the talk of the fair. The devotee of Baba Lokenath felt a deep urge to have his darshan (personal, one-to-one time with a saint). But there were thousands of people waiting to see him! How could he move through the large crowd?

Something within prompted him to put forth the effort. Driven by an unseen power, he reached the feet of the saint and prostrated himself with all his love and devotion. While prostrated, the picture of Baba Lokenath fell on the ground. When he quickly picked it up, the saint noticed and stretched out his hand to see the picture. The devotee handed it to him. The aged saint looked into the picture in a state of ecstasy. Lovingly he called the devotee closer and asked, "My child! Where did you get this picture?" The devotee's heart was full of joy. He was overwhelmed that the saint would be so interested in his Guru as to ask about him. In a voice choked with tears and love for his Guru, he said, "Oh! Holy One, this picture is of my Guru, who lived in a small village called Baradi, near Dacca (Bangladesh), for twenty-six years."

Filled with ecstasy, the saint exclaimed in amazement, "One who has these divine eyes and such a divine physical form, cannot come down from the Himalayas and live in human society. Blessed you are, blessed is your life, that you could see such a great yogi with your eyes, sit in his divine presence, talk to him or listen to his nectarine words."

Having said this, the saint went into samadhi, a state of deep, blissful absorption in the Divine, with Baba's picture in his hands. After a while he returned to this world and returned the picture to the devotee, saying, "All glory to the Guru, all glory to the Guru."

SRI VIJAY KRISHNA GOSWAMI

After traveling on foot to many pilgrim centers and meeting a number of living saints all over India, one of the great saints of India, Sri Vijay Krishna Goswami, came to Baradi. His experience there is a wonderful example of the Divine Play of Baba.

Baba was sitting in his small cottage at the Baradi ashram with a number of devotees surrounding him. As Vijay Krishna Goswami came in, he stood at the threshold of the hermitage and went into an ecstatic trance upon seeing Baba. In that state of divine intoxication, he told the others present, "Oh! All the gods and goddesses are in the body of Baba Lokenath! Celestial radiant beings are all around in the cottage praising him. He is Divine."

The scene was reminiscent of a child returning to its mother after a long absence. Baba left his seat to welcome Vijay with loving, outstretched arms. Vijay fell devotedly at Baba's feet; then Baba lifted him up and embraced him. One of the witnesses reported seeing a bright light flow from Baba's eyes into Vijay's body, as Vijay trembled in Baba's arms like a leaf blown by the wind. The whole cottage reverberated with an ecstatic sound coming from Vijay. It was like the Ganges coming to meet the sea. The individuality of Vijay merged in the ocean of love to be reborn into a life of eternal light.

The devotees present stood as stunned and speechless witnesses to this unique meeting of supernatural souls, overwhelmed by the miraculous power of Baba and his compassion. When Baba returned to meditation, Vijay's devotees caught his limp body and sat him down in front of Baba.

Touched by the transforming Divine Grace of Baba Lokenath, Vijay Krishna Goswami reached a very high state of yoga. As a Satguru, he initiated thousands of seekers into the path of yoga. Throughout his life, Prabhupada Vijay Krishna Goswami preached to his disciples about Baba's Divinity and yogic powers. Wherever he went, he spoke highly of Baba:

"I have never met a saint like Baba Lokenath. In Baba's body I have seen the manifestation of all the Divine beings of the celestial worlds. I have seen in him the three different forms of the Divine Mother, Gayatri, during dawn, midday, and dusk.

"Brahmachari Baba (Baba Lokenath) is totally free and self-willed. He can leave his body this moment or retain his body for any length of time, as he wishes."

In Sanskrit, "*Avangmansogocharah*" means that state where words and the mind fail to reach. The state which Baba Lokenath reached through his arduous penance is beyond words and mind. These two exalted, enlightened yogis help us at least to appreciate Baba's divine achievement, his unfathomable love and compassion for us. To attempt to reach him, we are like ants trying to climb to the moon. Yet reach we must, however great the distance, however impossible it may seem. The essence of Hindu philosophy is being and becoming. To know a saint, one has to become a saint. To see God, one has to become God. To know the Truth, one has to become One with the Truth. This is the difference between material and spiritual wisdom. In the material world, the knower and the object of knowledge always remain separate. In the realm of spirit, however, the knower, the object of knowledge, and knowledge itself all merge into one. Oneness is the ground of being of the spirit. It is the ultimate reality of spirit.

Baba freely dispensed the fruit of his long years of intense austerities. His word or touch removed the suffering of the multitudes that came to him. As Bhagwan Ganguly said of Baba, "In human life there is no higher state that can be reached."

From the loftiest heights of Nirvikalpa Samadhi (the state of absolute merger with the Divine), Baba descended to the earthly plane purely and simply to relieve suffering, to redeem souls caught and crying in the darkness of their separation from the Divine. He invites us to join him in that divine work of compassion. By making ourselves available to the fullness of the grace he came to bestow, by opening our hearts in loving service to all those who suffer, we respond to his invitation. It is a two-fold process.

Today, Baba is no longer in his physical body. He is the Divine Presence, the Presence working silently in the hearts of all those devoted to him. In his words:

> *"I have everything in me. What you need in life, you have only to take."*

> *"Do not think with the death of this body everything will come to an end. I shall be as available to you as I ever was when in my physical body. Only this body will be burnt to ashes. That 'I' which is not the body will never perish. I am that Changeless, Immutable One. I am never lost nor finished. Wherever and whenever anybody needs my help, I shall be available forever after."*

MEDITATION

Ponder in prayer: What could it mean to my life to take Baba's promise literally? Am I willing to take his promises to heart, to trust them absolutely, to rely on them, and call on Baba's loving help in all the dangers I face, inner as well as outer?

What limits me, day-in and day-out? What faults, what addictions, what habits of thinking, behaving and relating undermine my experience in the Divine? What physical dangers threaten me?

Make a complete list. Then call on Baba sincerely, as a lost and vulnerable child. Talk to him as a loving father and mother, in detail, about each one. Pray for his help in utterly resolving each issue. Then lay yourself open to the flow of Divine Grace and inspiration. Reread his promises regularly, whenever you are in any kind of difficulty, and call on his saving grace, again and again.

CHAPTER 2

A LIFE DEDICATED TO THE DIVINE FROM BIRTH

BABA LOKENATH WAS born in 1730 in the remote village of Chourasi Chakla (north of Calcutta) in West Bengal. His father, Ram Narayan Ghosal, was a devout Brahmin, who spent much of his time meditating and studying the scriptures. His mother, Kamala Devi, was calm, quiet, serene and pure of heart.

Sannyasin (the order of Hindu monks) in India have always been revered by all classes of society. Most Hindus of that time believed that if one member of a family renounced the world to become a sannyasin, then the entire family would be liberated from the wheel of incarnation. Ram Narayan, a staunch Hindu, had faith in this popular belief and told his wife that he wanted their first-born son to become a sannyasin.

Kamala Devi, in the Hindu tradition of a faithful wife, silently accepted the wish of her husband. When the first son was born, however, although the wife had promised, the new mother could not keep her word. The convincing logic of Ram Narayan fell on deaf ears. Kamala Devi could not bring herself to abandon her precious child to a life that promised such austerity and uncertainty.

Ram Narayan's trust in the Divine Will was undeterred, even when Kamala Devi would not relinquish either of the two sons who followed. Taking refuge in the power of prayer, Ram Narayan continued to pray for the fulfillment of his intention. At last his prayers were heard. The time was ripe for his dream to come true. A fourth son was born.

Those attending the birth reported signs of Grace from the very beginning of Baba's life. A light shown all around the baby as he sat on Kamala Devi's lap. Kamala Devi's face radiated with a divine glow. Ram Narayan, standing on the threshold of the labor room, was lost in trance looking at the child. Drawn to Baba's magnetic eyes, Ram Narayan felt a holy purpose in the child's birth. Kamala Devi, with a sublime smile, gave her consent to surrender her newborn to the Divine.

When Lord Krishna was born in prison, the iron gates opened by themselves and the guards fell unconscious. So, too, with the birth of Kamala Devi's fourth child, the gates of attachment unlocked themselves. The bonds of *Maya* (illusion) were released. The holy mother rose above her attachment to the child and surrendered him for the redemption of the world.

The mother who does not bind her child with the fetters of her own attachment, one who allows the child to follow its true path of spiritual awakening, is an ideal mother. In this sense, the Enlightened Ones are all mothers. They love their devotees as children, but they love without attachment. They love with a love that allows growth and transformation into the highest fulfillment of life. The surrender of her fourth baby elevated Kamala Devi to the state of a truly spiritual mother.

Baba described his boyhood days to his disciple, Brahmananda Bharati, this way: *"In my boyhood days, my elderly kin would speak to me of the highest principles of the Vedas and of spiritual knowledge, so that I would develop a sense of renunciation and love for God. I used to listen patiently to their knowledgeable talks and spend the rest of the time playing with boys of my age. This is how I passed my boyhood days."* This statement indicates that Baba's parents did not send young Lokenath to school for formal, secular education. That did not, however, keep the unlettered boy, from one day becoming an embodiment of wisdom.

During Lokenath's early youth, a Vedic scholar named Sri Bhagwan Ganguly lived in the neighboring village. Ganguly was a scholar of great repute who was revered as a householder sannyasin. Ganguly was sixty years old and was second to none in knowledge of the scriptures. In all conferences and debates on scriptural injunctions throughout India, Bhagwan Ganguly's judgment was considered unexcelled and definitive. His knowledge of the scriptures was preeminent.

Ram Narayan approached Bhagwan Ganguly and asked him to become the Acharya Guru (the guru who initiates the adolescent boy into the Gayatri Mahamantra at a sacred thread ceremony and then leads him toward the ultimate realization of the Self).

Ganguly sensed a divine destiny in Lokenath when he heard the story of Ram Narayan's implacable prayers for a spiritual son and Kamala Devi's surrender of this, her fourth son. Bhagwan Ganguly intuited the immense potential with which Lokenath had come into the world -- to manifest the truth, once again, that God exists in seed form in the human soul and that, with the practice of spiritual discipline, transcendent Divinity will blossom in the extraordinary seeker.

Bhagwan Ganguly readily welcomed this unique opportunity. Through the sadhana of Lokenath, he could translate all of his theoretical knowledge of the *shastras* into practical reality. He could prove to the world the greatness and glory of *brahmacharya*, the practice of celibacy, and one-pointed devotion toward God. Ganguly was convinced that Lokenath was the proper soil in which to sow the seed of a yoga which combined Bhakti (the path of devotional surrender) and Jnana (the path of knowledge of the Will of the Divine).

Ram Narayan returned home, filled with gratitude to the All-Merciful God.

Bhagwan Ganguly agreed to perform the sacred thread ceremony when Lokenath reached the age of eleven. The most auspicious day was selected for the performance of the ceremony since it was decided that after the initiation, young Lokenath would start out on his journey with his teacher.

Lokenath's bosom friend, Benimadhav, whose sacred thread ceremony was also fixed on the same day, expressed his firm determination to leave home with Lokenath and Bhagwan Ganguly. Benimadhav's parents, however, were not willing to let him go and tried their best to dissuade him. They attempted to get the boy to see the seriousness of his decision, which was no longer child's play, by painting a dreadful picture of the lives of *sannyasin*, who must live in absolute uncertainty as far as the material demands of the body are concerned.

The warnings of his elders went unheeded and Benimadhav, undeterred, stepped into his larger destiny as the companion of Lokenath in the search for the Absolute. The matter was presented to Bhagwan Ganguly and, as the Divine willed, he agreed to perform the sacred thread ceremony for Benimadhav on the same day.

The news about the two young boys leaving home under the guidance of such a renowned scholar and householder, who by then had reached the age of sixty, spread quickly. People assembled in large numbers at the residence of Lokenath to witness the ceremony. The entire ceremony was conducted by Bhagwan Ganguly in accordance with scriptural injunctions and reminded the people of a *yajna*, or sacred fire ceremony, which was performed in the ancient Vedic days.

It is important to note that Lokenath was not a brahmachari in the lineage of Adiguru Shankaracharya's sannyasin and brahmacharin. Guru Bhagwan initiated Lokenath and Benimadhav as Naisthic Brahmacharin. Unlike brahmacharin, who wear white clothes, Naisthic brahmacharin traditionally put on ochre colored robes and follow more orthodox rules of celibacy, food, etc.

Soon after the ceremony, Guru Bhagwan left with his two young disciples to live in the jungle. Thus, their spiritual odyssey in search of the Indwelling *Atman* began in the tradition of the Rishis of ancient Vedic times. Lokenath and Benimadhav walked happily alongside their new guardian. After traveling miles through villages and jungles, they reached Kalighat, a holy pilgrimage site in Calcutta which is the seat of Shakti, the Universal Mother.

A BRIEF HISTORY OF KALIGHAT AND CALCUTTA

The history of Kalighat in Calcutta and how the Deity of the Divine Mother Kali came to be worshipped there is noteworthy.

The story goes back more than a thousand years. At that time there were deep jungles at the bank of the Ganges before she merged into the Bay of Bengal. There were no roads. Only renounced monks, called *sadhus*, walked through these jungles on their way to the confluence of the Ganges and the Sea. This sacred mythological site is one of important place pilgrimage to millions of Hindus. Bathing, especially in the Ganges and Narmada Rivers, is a ritual of purification to all Hindus. Even westerners often come away stunned at the purifying and renewing power of bathing, or merely standing with their feet in the Ganges. And the Narmada purifies with only a glance.

The *sadhus* moved in large numbers to ensure security from the dangerous animals of the jungle. In spite of the group protection, however, many *sadhus* were lost to the jaws of tigers and crocodiles. On this occasion, a small group of *sadhus* were traveling through the jungle, playing musical instruments and loudly singing the Holy Name of God to scare away animals and to strengthen their faith in the Divine. The group found a place to rest after a long day's walk. The elder took a break under a big tree while others moved out in small groups to gather fruits, water, and wood for the night fire. One *sadhu* named Atmaram unknowingly moved deeper and deeper into the forest, away from his smaller group. Atmaram was a simple-hearted, true devotee. He found himself alone in a place which was incredibly peaceful, at a large lake with wonderful lotus flowers. Lost in the ecstatic fragrance of the lotus, he sat to meditate and effortlessly went into trance. In deep meditation, he saw a corner of the lake become bright with light. The light assumed the form of a radiantly Divine young girl, who spoke to him, saying, "My child! I am the Divine Mother Kali."

In even more ancient times, during the incarnation of Lord Shiva (the "Destroyer" of the Hindu Trinity), King Daksha, who was the father of Mother Durga (another form of Divine Mother and the wife of Lord Shiva), performed a great fire ritual to appease the gods. Daksha, however, did not invite Durga's husband, Lord Shiva, to attend the ceremony. Shiva — being a sannyasin — did not possess material wealth and Daksha did not approve of his ashen, unkempt and materially dispossessed son-in-law. Durga was deeply insulted. She fainted in the middle of the congregation.

Shiva saw this while in meditation and instantly appeared at the *yajna* site. He was furious. Lifting the body of Durga onto His shoulder, Shiva moved through the worlds in a rage with his third eye open and shooting fire, destroying everything along the way.

The other gods, afraid Shiva would annihilate the entire universe, prayed to Lord Vishnu, the Sustainer, to stop Shiva. Vishnu threw his *sudarshandisk* and cut the body of Durga into pieces, stopping Shiva. Parts of Durga's pure and chaste body fell at different places, all of which subsequently became the most powerful Shakti temples of Divine Mother.

In Atmaram's vision, Kali revealed that one of the toes of Durga's right foot fell into this lake and had been preserved there ever since. Kali told Atmaram, "I want to manifest in this place as Dakshina Kali to bring all auspiciousness to the people of the world in this Kali

Yuga. Right now I am in the Nilgiri Mountains in the loving care of my devotee, Brahmananda. Go there and tell him about my wish to be brought here and installed as deity."

Atmaram emerged from his meditative trance remembering this divine command. Inspired by Mother's Vision he walked to the Nilgiri Mountains, where he found the great sage, Brahmananda, deep in meditation. Atmaram told Brahmananda about Mother Kali's instructions. The huge stone on which Brahmananda sat for meditation became a flying disk which carried him and Atmaram to the side of the lake. Thoroughly searching the corner of the lake of Atmaram's vision, they found the Divine Mother Durga's toe, now in stone form.

Mother Kali then came to Atmaram in another dream. She instructed him to carve the black stone on which they had flown from the mountains into a new form of the Deity, hiding the toe inside it, and to worship it as Mother Kali. Brahmananda and Atmaram took a long time and great care to carve a beautiful image of Mother Kali. A small cottage was built to install the Deity for regular worship.

Brahmananda and Atmaram thus became instrumental in founding the Kali Temple and installing Mother Kali's idol. The small triangular island on the lake, which became the energy field of Mother Kali, came to be known as Kalighat. Ghat refers to the bank of a river. Most of the merchants who passed by that way to go to the sea stopped there to offer their respects to the Mother. Because the Mother's temple was situated at the bank of the Ganges, it became popularly known as Kalighat.

Though no exact date or time could be said as to when this place first came to be known as Kalighat, research suggests that it was about a thousand years ago, during the Pal dynasty.

Towards the end of the sixteenth century A.D., during the regime of Mughal Emperor Akbar, Abul Fazal wrote Ain E Akbari referring to the present area of Calcutta as 'Kalikotta.' In those days the area was only a jungle. The whole area was known as Kalighat -- there was no separate name. (Baba corroborated this.) Abul Fazal, while writing 'Kalighat' in the Persian language, wrote it as 'Kalikotta.' Later, the same name uttered by the English traders took the form 'Calcutta.' Hence, the name 'Calcutta' was derived from 'Kalighat.'

Kalighat made an appropriate setting for Baba and Beni to come to approach Divine Mother for darshan and to receive her blessings before starting decades of rigorous austerities and yoga practices.

In the words of Baba, *"At that time (1742), Calcutta was no more than a jungle, and Kalighat, the temple of Mother Kali, stood in the midst of a wild forest. The English traders, who had not yet established their kingdom in India, conducted their trade in and around Kalighat. When we arrived there, we found it was populated by a large number of sannyasin with long locks of matted hair. Beni and I found their company most enjoyable. Within a few days we started feeling quite at home in Kalighat. When the sadhus sat silently in meditation, we, in childish playfulness, would pull their long hair or touch their loincloths. They never said anything to us. This encouraged us and we continued disturbing them off and on.*

"When the disturbance reached its peak, the sannyasin approached Guru Bhagwan to complain about our misbehavior. Gurudev answered

them, 'Why do you complain to me? I am a householder. These boys belong to your Ashram. I am only instrumental in bringing these two boys, belonging to your order, from home to you." The sannyasin, pleased by this apt reply, did not complain anymore. The episode was over. Gurudev called us to his presence, and said sweetly, "You are pulling the long hair and the loincloths of the sannyasin. When you, too, have grown old and others pull your long, matted hair or pull your loincloths, then what will you do?"

"I said, 'How strange! We wear the long clothes given to us on the day of the sacred thread ceremony. Why on earth would we grow long hair and put a bit of loincloth around our waist?"

"Gurudev replied, 'Don't you understand by now that you are to become like these renounced monks?"

"I replied, 'If we have come to be like them, then, why do they live on alms and we on the money sent from our homes?' Gurudev said, 'Even that money should be treated as received in alms. The people at home know our address, hence, they send money for our expenses.' When I heard this, I told Gurudev, 'If that is the case, we should not stay here anymore. We should immediately move to a distant place.' Gurudev readily agreed to my suggestion, and we left Kalighat."

With respect to Gurudev, Baba Lokenath explained to his devotees and disciples, *"Gurudev would always put me in the forefront whenever we were able to move to a new place or when a new venture was to be undertaken."*

Lokenath, at just eleven years old, requested that they leave Kalighat to avoid depending on money from home and live as true wandering mendicants. We see in this his inherent tendency toward renunciation. Baba was a born yogi. We also see in Gurudev's response to such requests a training for and deference to Lokenath's leadership. In allowing Baba's leadership to express and develop early, Gurudev foreshadows Lokenath's destiny.

MEDITATION

Sitting comfortably erect for meditation, offer all that you are into the rising and falling light within the breath. When you are deeply relaxed, see yourself before you were born, as a spark of diamond-white light in the Divine Heart. Feel the pure, sweet, nurturing energies of the Divine all around you, like a womb. Feel the pure essence of the Divine as your own essence. This is home, where you come from, who you are beyond form. Allow the golden-white, Divine Light to flow through you now, informing and forming your life today in ways that are beyond your understanding. Wrapped in the Light that is your true home, know that you are safe, that you can always return to this Light, because it is who you are. Everything else will one day disappear. Only this Light will be left. Whenever you are beset with difficulty, remember this simple, brilliant spark of Light that you are. Offer your troubles into it. Let the Light burn them away until they disappear into the Light.

CHAPTER 3

A RIGOROUS DISCIPLINE OF YOGA

Guru Bhagwan and his young brahmacharins resumed their wandering once again and headed toward an unknown destination. Guru Bhagwan preferred to live in a forest area that was somewhat populated, so that he could beg for food while guiding his students on the path of active spiritual discipline.

Guru Bhagwan foresaw the magnitude of enlightenment that Lokenath was to achieve. He developed a protracted program of yogic disciplines designed to prepare Lokenath's body for the full measure of the Divine Grace that was to descend on him. With this sole objective, Bhagwan implemented yogic disciplines designed to develop self-restraint from yielding to basic bodily desires. Coupled with hatha yoga for a period of thirty to forty years, these practices honed Baba's body, mind, heart, and will for what was to come.

Guru Bhagwan guided the brahmacharins through the most arduous practices of hatha yoga in order to establish full control of the physical functioning and vital energies of the body. Baba expressed very little about the details of this part of his practice, which extended over 35 years. In "*Sri Sri Satguru Sanga*," however, we have the written account of Kuladananda Brahmachari, who had the privilege of close proximity to Baba. Kuladananda recorded all that he heard from Baba in his personal diary, which was subsequently published in five volumes in Bengali. Kuladanananda, who was to become a great saint of eastern India, recorded Baba's comments on the austerities of hatha yoga: "*...hereafter my Guru took me to a hilly region and made me practice hatha yoga for a period of 35 years. When I became more interested in the practice of raja yoga, my Guru tested my mastery of the hatha practices, saying, 'You have to cook sweet rice pudding by placing a pot in between the upper parts of your legs and offer that to me.' I did as my Guru asked. Then he started giving me lessons on raja yoga. It took a long time for me to perfect raja yoga.*"

FASTING

Guru Bhagwan knew that the foundation of integral yoga is Brahmacharya, which involves strict observance of the vow of celibacy and conservation of energy for transmutation into Ojas, the energy for spiritual enlightenment. During this 35-year period, Baba and Benimadhav went through a vow of fasting called Naktabrata. Nakta in Sanskrit means night. The observance of this vow calls for fasting during the day and taking light food at night.

When Guru Bhagwan determined that Lokenath and Benimadhav had mastered Naktabrata, he started them on Ekantara. Ekantara is fasting for two days and taking some light food on the second night. After Ekantara, Triratri was practiced, which involved fasting for three days and taking food on the third night. The next vow was Panchaha, fasting for five days and taking food on the fifth night. This vow was followed by Navaratri, with fasting for nine consecutive days and taking food on the ninth night.

After the completion of the vow of Navaratri, Lokenath and Benimadhav began Dwadashah, which calls for fasting for twelve days and breaking the fast on the twelfth night.

This vow of Dwadashah was continually practiced for an extended period. With the success of this vow, they graduated to the next vow of Pakshah, which required fasting for fifteen days and having food on the fifteenth night. Both of the brahmacharins successfully performed this difficult vow and finally qualified for the most difficult, Masabrata, fasting for one month. Baba Lokenath told his devotees that the Masabrata was performed twice. He fasted successfully both times, but Benimadhav could not complete the second vow.

Each of these vows was repeated over long periods totaling thirty to forty years. However unbelievable it may seem to the modern scientific mind that the human body could withstand such austerities, there is a long tradition of yogic techniques which enabled the young brahmacharins to carry out these arduous practices.

During this long period of sadhana, Guru Bhagwan tended to his disciples' every need. Leaving the brahmacharins in the jungle, he would go to a nearby village to beg alms from householders. Upon his return, he would prepare a special diet of boiled milk and seasamum (sesame seeds). After serving it to the brahmacharins, he would take the same food for himself. According to the Master, this was the best diet for brahmacharins. Reminiscing about his early days of sadhana, Baba told his devotees, *"After having this wonderful diet every day for a long time, we got so fed up with it that the very sight of milk and seasamum would irritate us, and we wondered why the householders did not offer us any other food in alms."*

Despite their irritation, neither Lokenath nor Benimadhav ever expressed their feelings about the food. They had surrendered unconditionally to Guru Bhagwan and accepted whatever was offered to them without complaint.

When the brahmacharins had grown quite strong and able-bodied, they approached Guru Bhagwan and said, *"We are no longer able to accept the idea of sitting in the jungle with our young and energetic bodies while you go to distant villages to beg alms from the villagers."* Guru Bhagwan was touched by the concern of his disciples but convinced them otherwise by saying, "No, if you are allowed to do that, the single-pointedness of your minds will become disturbed. If you expose yourselves to the activities and ways of householders, there is a danger that you will develop such tendencies in your minds. You must understand that there is always the possibility of a fall from the yogic state that you have reached through your long spiritual discipline."

On another occasion, Lokenath had an understandable doubt and innocently presented it to his Gurudev. Baba asked Guru Bhagwan, *"Knowledge of the scriptures is supposed to be a part of the discipline of a spiritual aspirant. Why, then, is Gurudev simply indifferent about this aspect, in spite of the fact that he himself is a respected scholar in all the schools of Vedic philosophy?"*

Gurudev replied, "Why should you take the pains of learning the shastras? I have studied a great deal. You need not take those pains. Why should you waste your time reading bundles of worn-out, torn papers? Whenever you need the guidance from any of the scriptures, you can always receive it from me.

"Instead of wasting time acquiring borrowed knowledge from books, utilize that time in the practice of yoga. If you know who you are, you will come to know everything. There is nothing in this external, manifested world which is not within you. Believe my words; there is no truth without, because your *Atman* is *'sarvabhutatman,'* the *Atman* seated in the hearts of all creatures. In you is the dormant seed form of all the knowledge, power, and wealth of this entire creation. Why should you leave the diamond and waste time on pieces of glass?"

Lokenath continued, *"I thought this book knowledge was essential for our sadhana. Without it, how are we to find a place in the society of sages who are so well versed in Vedic literature?"*

Patiently, Gurudev convinced Lokenath by saying, "The discipline of yoga which I am giving to you through this strict observance of celibacy and fasting will, in due course, grant you profound knowledge, not only of the scriptures, but of everything that exists in this cosmos. This observance combined with the unalloyed trust you have in your Guru will allow all my scriptural knowledge to be transmitted to you without any study on your part."

Gurudev continued, "If you study the various shastras, then you are apt to become confused by the many contradicting opinions of the commentators, and the concentration of your mind will be disturbed. Apart from that, once you study the scriptures and form opinions in your own mind, you will not be able to accept my spiritual guidance as innocently and without complaint as before. You will always judge my instructions in the light of your borrowed, conditioned knowledge. This will hinder your spiritual growth, which is advancing steadily in your present state of clear, unconditioned mind. Knowledge that is borrowed always becomes a barrier to spiritual advancement."

Guru Bhagwan ended his argument by saying, "Your demand to learn the shastras without proper realization can make you a glorified pundit, a renowned scholar, or a grand philosopher, but never an Enlightened One. Follow my path and you will reach your goal."

Guru Bhagwan was a master with profound understanding of human psychology. He was not complacent in accepting the mere observance of the arduous fasting as sufficient for attaining spiritual awareness. He kept a vigilant watch on the play of the subconscious minds of the young brahmacharins. Not a single thought process went unnoticed. He would carefully observe their thoughts and channel their energies in the right direction. To this end, he designed techniques that would train the brahmacharins to keep ever awake and alert regarding the intricate play of their deeper minds.

While inspiring the young brahmacharins to practice continence sincerely, Guru Bhagwan also instructed the boys in the discipline of hatha yoga. On the path of Self-Realization, hatha yoga plays an important role. It is a practice by which the hatha yogi attains perfect control over the body and vital prana.

The body and mind are as closely related to each other as two sides of the same coin. Until the natural tamasic tendencies of the body are transformed, control of the mind is impossible. Because the body is the vehicle for the journey to the inner world, the seeker must first purify it through asana, pranayama, fasting, and other similar practices so that it becomes fit to carry the mind to its final destination, the state of no-mind.

The aim of yoga is the complete cessation of the mind. The body is like a container, or pot. The mind is like water. The slightest movement of the pot disturbs the stillness of the water. Therefore unless the body remains, through practice, in a state of rest, the mind within can never reach a state of tranquillity. The tranquil mind, through yogic practice, reaches the state of non-mind, which is the supreme state of samadhi, or total God Consciousness.

The severe austerities which Guru Ganguly devised for Baba and Benimadhav may seem extreme to our every day consciousness. They were, however, a totally appropriate preparation for the magnitude of Mastery, Grace and Light which Baba brought into the world.

THE ROLE OF THE SATGURU

Lokenath always choked with emotion when he spoke about Guru Bhagwan's motherly love during this long period of continence and fasting. He said, *"Gurudev would always be alert so that we did not need to move our bodies while we were seated at meditation during this fasting. We were not allowed to move, even while attending to the call of nature. Like a loving mother, he would wash away urine or stool and carry us to a clean place. He would then remove the stool, throw it a distance away, and then finally clean the whole place."*

Those present with Baba at Baradi said that Baba cried profusely when telling about the tenderness of his Guru's care for him. The assembled devotees were so moved that they, too, found it difficult to restrain their emotions. The love that Guru Bhagwan had for his two young disciples is indeed a rare and unforgettable example of the Guru-disciple relationship. And the devotion that Baba Lokenath returned to his Master was intense and complete.

The need for a Guru in spiritual life has often been questioned the world over. One valid reason is the fear that has been created by the false gurus in the marketplace of spiritual seekers. The large number of sects and the stories of abuses of spiritual power which are circulated in the news media from time to time have legitimately contributed to guru-phobia, especially in those who are unfamiliar with Hindu tradition.

There are others who are open to a Guru, but who remain confused as to who is the right one. Whatever the reason for the present day guru-phobia and the attendant indifference towards the need for the Guru in spiritual life, the truth remains unchanged. Realization of the Self and the need for the Satguru always go together. The Satguru — or True Guru — is one who has reached the highest of all goals: permanent and complete union with the Divine. The realized Master has gone though the process of nurturing the God-seed in his or her heart until it finally achieves mature flowering. He or she alone can become the true Master who has trod the path of Truth, successfully negotiating all the ups and downs of the spiritual path to reach the peak of enlightenment. The Enlightened Ones make themselves available to the seeker by Divine Will. As the embodiment of Divine Compassion for those of us who remain trapped in the illusion of separation, the Satguru lights the way. Without the Grace of such a master as a spiritual teacher, the path of Truth is like moving through the thickest jungle without a guide.

The scriptures and other spiritual books are invaluable. But the simple truth is, for the immature and struggling seeker, most often they are borrowed, encased in dead, distorted, ill-conceived or inherited interpretation, which limits our effective application of the wisdom they contain. It is the Conscious, living Divine, through the

Satguru, who gives us, as seekers, the wisdom, confidence and tools to find our way through the jungle to our final destination.

The Satguru guides from outside, in the form of a material person whose words can be heard, whose life and teachings are living manifestations of the Divine, and whose very presence opens the heart center to the Divine Light and music within. Drawing our attention to the emptiness of the material world and material relationships, the Satguru shows us the way home by creating situations which lead us within. Gradually, we realize that God alone is real and that we are God-Seed. From outside, the Satguru pushes us inward.

The Satguru also guides from within. Sitting within our own hearts, in the sanctum sanctorium, he or she pulls us back toward the center. That is why the Guru is also called the Antaryamin, the indwelling controller. S/he is the Conscience — the faculty of discrimination between the temporal/transient and the permanent/transcendent. The Sat is inseparable from Brahman, the Pure Conscious field. The Sat operates from within our own consciousness, making the larger, Divine Consciousness available to us (at whatever intensity we can sustain it) by virtue of His or Her inseparability from us and the Divine. Without the Grace of the Guru, no one can attain the state of Pure Mind.

How do we find such a Guru? We are essentially searchers. We keep searching for Truth, for the Master, for the One in whose presence all our questions — and our bubbling minds — will find rest. Through the Guru, we find unspeakable peace. In the Guru's presence, all of our so-called knowledge, all our pretensions, gradually pale into insignificance. We become possessed by a deep feeling of inner silence and spontaneous meditation. Our questions are answered without the need to ask them. With sincere searching and prayer, we prepare ourselves for the Guru, who comes to us when we are ready.

Lokenath exemplifies to the world how, by the path of surrender, the disciple can reach the highest peak of spiritual attainment. Guru Bhagwan exemplifies the deepest of all loves, the love that the Guru always possesses for a true disciple.

No relationship in the world can be compared with the Guru-disciple relationship. All ordinary, worldly relationships give us pleasure and happiness. But they can never give us the wisdom of the Self. All relationships are ties which subtly fetter and bind the soul. Even the best and healthiest human relationships bring pain, misunderstanding, and conflict that often go unresolved. They cannot give us true freedom. Freedom, ultimately, is a state of mind where there is no attachment to anything or anybody. It is antithetical to the concepts of caring which are important to us in human relationships. It is the Guru alone who can take the child, holding his/her hands through the most arduous and subtle paths of the Spirit, to the true realization of freedom. The Guru is the One who releases the disciple from the bondage of what we collect from human birth. The Guru releases the disciple from the painful chain of karma, which binds all souls until true freedom is achieved.

Baba was a truly surrendered disciple who was capable of grasping the magnitude of the gift of the Satguru in his spiritual life. That is the reason Baba cried like a small child whenever he had anything to say about his Guru. Baba was the embodiment of Guru-bhakti (love towards one's own Guru).

When speaking of his early days in the practice of yoga, Baba demonstrates the subtlety of the Guru's guidance and the importance of the Guru's wisdom in understanding when to apply what lesson or practice. Baba Lokenath talked further about the practice of yoga in his earlier days. *"During the initial days of the practice of continence, we would always be kept in isolation; but toward the end, Gurudev did just the reverse. He would take us to crowded market places to sit in meditation. When we found the commotion a disturbance to our concentration and brought this to Gurudev's attention, he would say, 'Just as you have practiced concentration of mind in isolation, so must you also reach a state of deep meditation while sitting in the midst of the disturbing interference of people.' Then we started practicing meditation while sitting in such marketplaces, in accordance with his instructions.*

"In the same manner, Gurudev made us learn to patiently endure the bites of ants and mosquitoes and other insects while we practiced meditation. Once, when we were practicing yoga in a jungle, I told Gurudev, 'Here the ants are very disturbing elements to our peaceful meditation. Why do we not move to some other place?' Then I sat in a meditative posture with my eyes closed and pretended that I was meditating. To my utter surprise, Gurudev was inviting the ants by throwing sugar around the place of our meditation! Then I understood that the intention of Gurudev was to give us a state of mind that could not be perturbed either by shouting crowds or by the bites of insects. In fact, afterwards we would become deeply absorbed in meditation by totally withdrawing our senses from their contact with the external, objective world."

Baba was circumspect in revealing the details of his long periods of fasting. Few were privy to those experiences, since he felt that the average person would not understand them. Baba simply said, *"The impossible is not expressed."* He was always opposed to any publicity about his life and sadhana. Only his closest disciples and devotees could draw from him some of the experiences of his early days of spiritual discipline.

Once, Premananda Bharati (who became popularly known in America as Baba Bharati) was deeply moved by the spiritual influence of this yogi and expressed his heart's desire to write a book on Baba Lokenath's Divine Life. He sat in front of Baba with pen and paper in hand and requested that Baba to speak to him about his life. Baba answered him harshly, *"What is so great about my life? Are not the Ramayana and Mahabbharata enough? How many people have become like Rama and Laxmana by the study of the Ramayana? How many people have become as virtuous and truthful as Yudisthira by the study of the Mahabbharata? How many Prahlads and Dhruvas are born by the study of the Puranas? Take your pen and paper away from here! You need not write my life history. This is the place of command, not advice!"*

Although Lokenath admonished Premananda about writing a book on his life, there were occasions when Baba did speak about certain episodes in his early life. To Brahmananda Bharati, his direct disciple, he described one experience at length, which occurred while in a state of deep meditation during his second Masabrata.

BABA EXPERIENCES HIS PREVIOUS BIRTH

"In my inner mind I could see as if in a dream that the river Damodar was flowing through the district of Burdwan (West Bengal). On the bank of the river was a village of moderate size, Beruga by name. In that village, in the family of Bandopadhyay, I was moving about as Sitanath Bandopadhyay. When I told Gurudev about this experience, he immediately brought a pencil

and instructed me to write all about it, in exact detail. I did so accordingly. Long after this episode, we three set out on foot and when we reached an unknown place by the side of a river, Gurudev pointed to the village on the bank of the river and asked, 'Have you ever seen this place before?'

"I remembered all my visions during Masabrata and said, 'I wrote once about the Damodar River. It appears to be that river.' Then I recognized the village Beruga, as the three of us entered the village. I realized that the experience during Masabrata was not merely a dream but a flash of memories from my previous birth.

"The elderly people of Beruga who were still alive talked specifically about the life of Bandopadhyay. The more they talked, the more memories of the past came afresh to my mind. All that I saw and recorded on the day of the experience regarding Sitanath's father and about other members of his family was proven correct when the villagers also gave the same information on our inquiry."

Baba added further, *"The spontaneous recollection of the memories of the previous birth was enhanced when I stayed in Beruga for a few days. As I focused my mind more on the memories of the past, more facts about my previous birth returned to the surface of the conscious plane, much like the memories from the earlier days of this birth."*

After further questioning, Baba said, *"I could clearly remember in detail all that I did as Sitanath during his life and after his death until I once again took birth from my mother's womb in this present birth."*

Usually those who are Jatishmara (persons remembering past lives) by birth remember all of their past lives spontaneously. This was not so in Baba's case. Baba knew nothing about this until that day while in samadhi during his second Masabrata.

In the 18th Sutra of Vibhutipada in Patanjali's Yoga Sutras, this aspect of spiritual experience is expressed thus, *"Samskara sakshat karanat pruvajati jnanena."* Through the practice of dharana, dhyana and samadhi, the yogi can attain knowledge of past births from the memories of the deeper mind. The experience which Baba achieved during his sadhana is a practical demonstration of this sutra.

After confirming the truth of Lokenath's remembrance of his previous birth, Guru Bhagwan left Beruga and took shelter in the nearby jungle. The brahmacharins were once again deeply absorbed in their spiritual quest.

MEDITATION

Prayerfully look back at all the effort you have made in your life to be a better person. Acknowledge your intense longing for the good and beautiful. Recall all that you have struggled to overcome in yourself and your circumstances. How often have you failed and started over? How discouraged have you felt? What grace has come along the way? How much darkness have you simply not been able to dispel despite constant effort? Realize it was never up to you alone, that our human darkness is too deep, too stubborn to be overcome without intimate guidance from one perfected in the light.

Ask Baba's help in finding your Guru if you do not have one. Ask him to bring you to the one to whom you can utterly surrender all your faults, the one whose pure light can bring you home to deep and abiding peace. If you have a Guru, pray now and deeply for complete surrender, surrender that will lead you all the way home. Then take deeply to heart all of Baba's teachings about the Guru-disciple relationship which are in this book.

CHAPTER 4

A LESSON IN MAYA

After completing the most rigorous and intricate disciplines of yoga, Guru Bhagwan returned with his disciples to their birthplace for the last time. This was in accordance with the injunction of the shastras, which states that after the completion of twelve years of renunciation, the sannyasin should return once more to the place of his birth.

While reminiscing about the days spent in his birthplace, Baba Lokenath revealed to his disciple, Narisababa, an important instruction on an aspect of human life that concerns every spiritual seeker. Narisababa gives a vivid account of what he heard from his Master on the issues of love and sex.

Baba Lokenath said, "*Love is beyond all human rationalization. The natural attraction between male and female has, too often, been viewed as immoral. But it is childish to give up sex or condemn it as a social evil. You have to go deep into this phenomenon to know its source. Why is this basic aspect of nature found in human beings? Why does man try, again and again, to rise above this instinctive urge, yet fail to succeed?*"

Then Baba gave the most practical explanation saying, "*To brand sex as a sin is the greatest blunder. How can that without which the creation is impossible be called a sin? Sin is a feeling of the mind in a state of unawareness. Sex cannot be separated from the world of desires. The hardships and material discomforts which a seeker of truth accepts happily to have the vision of God has its roots in desire. You may say that the desire for material pleasure is a limited one, whereas the desire for Divine Grace is of greater value in life, but can you deny the fact that at the root there is the phenomenon of desiring?*

"In man is the seed of desire; hence, there is the possibility of divine transformation. In the animal kingdom this sphere of desire is limited; therefore, the scope for divine illumination is not there. If you cannot desire the part, how can you grow and desire the whole? The entire creation is created with a divine design. It has its own inner harmony growing toward ultimate perfection. Nothing that is created is without deep significance. From the limited world of the material plane to the highest realms of spiritual oneness everything is a part of the divine design of the Supreme One. It is only through the desire for the transient objects of material life that the higher desire for spiritual flowering will awaken in the heart of man.

"The whole secret of this cosmic creation is hidden deep within this phenomenon of Kama or desire or sex. You may rail against this. You may try to suppress this natural urge, but that is to do the impossible. It is not possible to reach the state of divine love through the suppression of sex.

"Your material life and the natural tendency of desiring material happiness is divinely designed to take you to a state of higher evolution. Through this material desiring you reach a stage where, through the Grace of the Divine, when the time is ripe, your mind turns towards God and His Glory. Your sexual energy changes and transforms itself into love for the Divine and you then transcend desire in the world of Bliss."

Baba told Narisababa a memorable story from his life which clearly illustrates this important teaching.

Lokenath returned to his birthplace after years of observing his vow of celibacy. He had passed through the various disciplines of yoga undisturbed by any kind of social interference. The Divine Mother had taken Her dear child through the difficult path of austerity, but Lokenath had no experience with the world of Maya. Therefore, She prepared a lesson that would enrich him with the experience of attachment and sensual pleasure. Although Lokenath would transcend these experiences, he found himself faced with the most difficult test of his life.

When the two young brahmacharins, reached their native village, accompanied by the old master, the news of their arrival spread rapidly. Villagers came from all directions to welcome the returning sadhus. With great respect and devotion, people came forward with the little they had to offer to the sadhus and served them with all their hearts.

In India, sadhus and sannyasins have always been given the highest esteem in all classes of society. Particularly in the villages, where the illiterate population relies on belief. Imagine the sensation evoked by the return of the two sannyasins and the old Guru after such a long span of time. In the 1750s, villagers were simple and innocent. Everyone rejoiced at the return of the monks. People from far and wide came to have the darshan of the sannyasins, bringing offerings of fruit, milk and other edibles to the monks, who were seated under a huge banyan tree beside the village lake.

The traditional return to their native place, after twelve years of sannyas life, has a dual purpose. It allows the renunciate to pay respects to what and from whom he comes. At the same time, it tests the level of detachment achieved through yogic disciplines. Guru Bhagwan followed the tradition of bringing the celibates to their own village to experience for themselves the state of their own minds.

One of Baba's childhood playmates, who was now a young widow, came forward to offer her services to Lokenath. She immediately recognized him. The memories of their playful days were still clear in her mind. She appealed to Guru Bhagwan for his permission to serve Lokenath and Gurudev granted it without hesitation. Innocent and simple-hearted, Lokenath never suspected that this was the plan of Mahamaya, the Universal Mother. Day after day, the young woman served Lokenath with untiring devotion and won her own place in Lokenath's heart. The young woman began feeling a deep sense of attachment for the young sannyasin. Lokenath, with no wrong intention, felt the simple surrender and sincerity of the young woman very touching. They once again became close friends, enjoying each other's company.

Lokenath, being drawn by the illusive potency of Maya, felt the company of this woman harmless and at the same time delightful. He didn't realize the relationship was moving beyond friendship and gaining ground in his heart. Whenever he sat for meditation, it was not as easy as it was when he was practicing in the forests. In the wild, he could meditate for hours without any distractions or disturbance. Now, though his body was still, his mind was unsteady.

Unconsciously, his mind would move to memories of the woman and the talks they shared. He felt deeply connected to her. The attraction was a formidable state of mind to overcome, despite having previously been able to control his mind in more difficult situations. At times he would give up his practice and go to meet her.

Guru Bhagwan saw and understood everything. He knew that Lokenath had to pay his old debts to this woman. This is a karmic inevitability through which every human soul—however highly evolved—has to pass. Guru Bhagwan knew that Lokenath was not born to be permanently attached to the bondage of flesh or to this simple-hearted but noble village woman. This was a temporary drama of the Divine Mother, who wanted both to pass through their mutual karma and transcend beyond their sense of attachment.

The Guru pretended to know nothing, yet he subtly played with his beloved disciple. We can see what an open-hearted Master Guru Bhagwan was. Whenever he saw Lokenath struggling with his mind in meditation, Guru Bhagwan would ask him to go take a walk, or to talk to the villagers and take it easy. At times, he would advise his disciple to sense the Divine Play of Maya and consciously go through it without fighting against it.

At this stage, we see that the ways of a true Master are inscrutable! This was the same Master who took great pains during the previous years of penance, fasting, and celibacy to go to distant villages and beg alms. He boiled seasamum and milk without allowing the celibates to go to the villages, lest they fall prey to alluring situations. This was the same Guru who was extraordinarily careful and possessive of every moment through the protracted disciplines of hatha yoga.

Why did the same Guru knowingly allow Lokenath and this woman to feel closer to each other? The answer to that question is a clear demonstration of the need of the Guru in spiritual life. The

Guru alone knows what situations to create in order to purge the inner *sanskaras* (dormant tendencies) and to give practical experience to the disciple in rising above the deep seated roots of attachment. Every individual in this world is original. No two Buddhas are alike, other than in their state of *Samadhi Prajna* (Cosmic Unity Consciousness). The path of spirituality may appear similar on the surface, but every person is born to travel the path precisely through his or her own nature.

Guru Bhagwan knew that Lokenath came to demonstrate that one could come through all human weakness, rise above it, and reach Buddhahood to bring solace to millions of suffering souls.

In the lives of most great saints, we only read the stories of their practice, their purity, and sacrifice. We can't imagine them struggling with flaws and behaviors similar to our own. Our minds have fixed, preconceived ideas of purity and perfection in the lives of great saints. Those preconceptions give rise to self-condemnation, making us feel unfit for the light and grace with which God draws us closer to the Divine. Feeling we don't deserve God's grace, much less intimacy and Oneness with the Divine, we fall away, discouraged from the pursuit of the Divine, believing it is unattainable.

There are always priests and pseudo-religious teachers who reinforce guilt and condemnation in the devotee. They hold forth pure and perfect images of the lives of saints and sages. That a human emotional manifestation is possible in the life of a great spiritual Master is inconceivable to them.

Baba Lokenath's life, in all of its details, is formed by Providence. It inspires us to reach for the ultimate destiny of human existence, wherever we are. If Baba could feel such deep attachment to a woman after taking a vow of celibacy, after years of intensive hatha yoga and other yogic practices, why should a practicing seeker who falls prey to the same Maya become disheartened? Baba Lokenath's example of finally transcending this trial to become an exemplary Himalayan yogi is an invitation to one and all to forsake all self-condemnation. Resolve, with the Grace of the Divine and Baba, that you, too, can perfect yourself on the path home to God.

Let us hear all about this episode in Baba's life as he once described it to his dear devotee, Kuladananda Brahmachari, who recorded it in his personal diary, which was subsequently published under the title *"Sri Sri Satguru Sanga."*

Baba said, *"It was my fate that my Guru brought me to a place where a young widow lived. Guru would often go away from the place where we lived. That gave me the chance to spend time with that young girl and have a lot of fun. This went on for a period of almost three years. Gradually, my urge in that area of life began to diminish. Suddenly I had the deep thought 'What am I doing? Have I renounced my parents and home and come with this Holy Master for all these trifles?' I felt a deep sense of frustration. I started requesting of my Guru that we move to another place without further delay. For quite a few days, he paid a deaf ear to my requests. Later, he intentionally delayed the move by saying, ' We will go tomorrow.' My deep urge to leave the place increased. When I became adamant and strong in my decision, Gurudev pretended to be sick.*

"One day I felt an uncontrollable urge to leave. In a harsh manner, I said, 'I cannot stay here for another moment.' Guru said, 'I am feeling very sick, we will stay here for two more days.' Blind with anger, I took a big stick in my hand and ran towards my Guru saying, 'Whenever you

move in the village, or beg alms, or even cook for us, you don't feel sick. But the moment I say, 'Let us move from this place,' you start feeling ill. Today I will kill you and kill myself too.' My old Master ran away, but soon returned and said, 'Let's go, now it has happened.'

"When we started moving out of the village, I asked Gurudev, 'All these days you did not care what I said. Why did you listen to me today?' My Guru said, 'You never said it the way you did it today, my child. You had given up pleasures but the pleasures and the attachments did not give you up. Today it has happened.'"

This important statement by Guru Bhagwan needs deep contemplation. It is extremely common for all human beings to realize that our attachments lead to unhappiness in our lives. People at all levels of sadhana struggle to give up myriad habits, which they know cause pain for themselves and others, and which obstruct the internal peace which is the foundation of real spiritual progress. Most often, even though the habit is given up, it returns -- sometimes more vigorously. In spite of the firmest resolutions, even yogis in a high state of achievement fall. Until one is fully and naturally established in the state of egolessness and desirelessness, many possibilities to fall are open. That is why the *Upanishads* (the Vedas) liken the path of spirituality to one of walking on a razor's edge. The *Bhagavad Gita* tells us that this illusive *Maya* is insurmountable without the Grace of God and Guru.

Guru Bhagwan's wisdom in allowing Lokenath the time to fully release his karma reminds us that it is not enough to just give up anything that appears to cause us pain and unhappiness. The tendencies that manifest in the mind are rooted in the seeds of karma that the soul carried to this body. As circumstances and situations become more and more provocative, the inner, dormant tendencies of desire awaken. They stretch out their tentacles to draw the object of pleasure within reach until the desire is fulfilled. As the desires are again and again quenched the thirst increases, beginning the cycle again.

The ingrained seeds of karma work themselves out through a natural process and, eventually, the thirst for the pleasure diminishes. As the seeker passes through stages of cause and effect, experiencing the inner and outer consequences of attachment, the need to awaken to higher truths asserts itself. The longing gradually becomes paramount for deeper peace and harmony than is available through material desire and its fulfillment. Through the Grace of God and Guru, the seeker's determination to give up the unwanted desires becomes resolute. Her/his efforts become more powerful and single-pointed. They draw the Guru's grace to be able to rise above the karma. This is exactly what happened in Lokenath's case. Guru Bhagwan remained a witness to Lokenath's process, allowing and guiding it until the disciple exhausted the seeds of karma through his own efforts.

One need not feel that the young girl was abandoned by Lokenath after their karma together was burned. Just as Lokenath had to work out his karma, the girl also had to realize that any relationship with a renounced monk was against the norm of their society. It would only have led to more unhappiness in her life. She received Lokenath's company and friendship as long as the debts on both sides were being paid. In Hindu society of the Eighteenth Century, widows had to lead a life of renunciation, following a vegetarian diet, and strictly observing celibacy. Love and devotion to God were their only comfort. The company of Lokenath ultimately inspired the God-seed in her. Lokenath moved ahead on the path of truth as a wandering mendicant. The woman, transformed by the touch of a sannyasin, offered her life to the Divine to reach the state of desirelessness.

MEDITATION

Desire offered into the Heart of Compassion: (Use sexual desire if it is problematic to you in any way.) Sit quietly. Go inward, in prayer, inviting Baba's presence. Ask for Baba's Grace in helping you with a desire that is troublesome to you. First, acknowledge the desire and the problems it causes you, the truth and strength of its existence in you. Accept it as a part of being human, as an opportunity for deeper surrender, and an occasion for grace.

With your eyes closed, experience the desire simply as energy moving through you. Let that energy flow freely through your body for a while in whatever intensity it assumes. Then imagine Baba's heart, the heart of infinite compassion, all around and inside you. Direct the energy of the desire, and all of the problems it brings you, into Baba's heart of Divine Compassion, surrendering as it disappears into the sweet essence of compassion for all. Then, whenever the desire recurs, repeat the process.

CHAPTER 5

SELF-REALIZATION AND DEVOTION TO GURU

AUSTERITIES IN THE HIMALAYAS

THE HIMALAYAS ARE a rarified field of pure Divine Energy. As the holiest ground in all of India, these mountains have drawn great seekers of eternal Truth from time immemorial. The peace and tranquillity of their untouched heights are ideal for the journey within to the Self. The greatest yogis and rishis, the true researchers of the science of life, have come in a steady and constant stream. There, the exquisite beauty of nature and pristine spiritual vibrations are conducive to the direct experience of the pure energy underlying all manifestation. The mind is spontaneously elevated, detached from the mundane trifles of everyday life, as outer nature influences and informs inner nature.

The sages and Satgurus who have lived and practiced in the Himalayas, as well as the infrequent few who reached their inaccessible caves, tell of meetings with yogis and rishis (seers of Truth) who are three to four hundreds years old. These great, ancient souls are ever lost in deep meditation. Oblivious to their body and to time, they remain absorbed in Cosmic Consciousness. They live in camouflaged caves at high altitudes so that only those pranayama siddhas (those having total mastery over their vital air) who are blessed by the grace of the Satgurus can reach them. The ongoing presence of these exalted sages in the Himalayas has intensified the spiritual energy field, which is why the Himalayas are considered the seat of spiritual culture for the world.

Leaving the native village, the three wandering monks proceeded toward the Himalayas. They walked the entire distance of more than a thousand miles. On their way they passed through many forests and jungles. In one place along the way, they met a mystic who could foretell the future. Lokenath asked the seer if he would be able to withstand the intense cold he would face in the snowy regions of the Himalayas and also if he would realize the Self in his lifetime. In reply to both of these questions, the mystic said, "You will realize the Self in this life while doing your sadhana (spiritual practice) in the Himalayas. Through yoga, you will learn to live in the snow without any physical problems." Lokenath was extremely happy and more deeply committed to the path and the goal than ever. After months of traveling on foot, they reached the Himalayas.

Lokenath, in his later life as the Realized One, spoke very little about the sadhana he performed during his forty long years in the Himalayas before attaining God-Realization.

Lokenath was born with ingrained tendencies of deep faith and love for the Divine. His subtle intelligence allowed him to absorb, through practice, the choice seeds which Guru Bhagwan had collected from his own deep study of the Upanishads, the Gita, and Patanjali Yoga, and then had lovingly sown in Lokenath's mind. But the most important quality of Lokenath's nature was his innocent and childlike surrender to his Guru. His surrender was beyond question, absolutely unconditional. It gave Guru Bhagwan fertile ground in which to experiment and bring his theories to full and practical manifestation.

SELF-REALIZATION

Traversing the diverse paths and disciplines of yoga, Lokenath reached the pinnacle of Realization. He attained the Self, the state of being one with the absolute ground of reality, at one with the Beloved. Transcending all duality and multiplicity, he became established in the non-dual ground of pure energy and pure being — a fully conscious witness to the Divine Play in all its myriad forms in the ecstatic dance of creation, preservation and annihilation.

To whom could Baba speak about this unique state of his mind? Who would understand his language of the beyond? At times, though, Baba did make the attempt. *"Words are such poor vehicles to express the inner experience. Any attempt to reduce it to words only belittles the Ultimate Truth. It is like a mute trying to express the taste of nectar."* Talking to his intimate devotees, Baba once said, *"When I am talking about that, I am not able to stay in touch with my body. When I think of that, I become that. I am detached from body consciousness. It is impossible to express this, the deepest feeling of ecstatic bliss, in human language.*

"Everything that exists in infinite creation exists within me. The whole universe is in me. I am existence beyond space, time, and causation. My existence is without beginning or end. I exist in eternal expansion. These words are not to be shared. That is the reason you see me spending time with householders, granting their mundane demands. Do not think that when I am busy with you in worldly matters that I lose touch with that blissful state. No. Whoever achieves that state can never fall from there. Nothing can ever again be seen in isolation. Everything is seen as an expression of the One. In variety is the taste of Unity.

"Because I eat, drink, attend to the call of nature, and live like any one of you, you think of me as one like you. Your greatest mistake is to

think of me as a body. How am I to explain who I am? Everyone is so involved in the fulfillment of small desires, unconscious, so forgetful of their true 'I'."

Baba Lokenath's expression of identification with Ultimate Truth flows like Divine music from the world beyond. It echoes the words of Lord Krishna in the *Bhagavad Gita*, "Ignorant people seeing Me in human form mistake Me for an ordinary human. They fail to realize that I am the Paramatman (God)." (Gita, 9.11)

There is also a Vedic text which explains Baba's state of yoga: "The One Divine Being is hidden in all beings. He is omnipresent, the Indwelling Self of all beings, the witness, the one who imparts consciousness, unconditioned and without qualities." (Svetasvatara Upanishad. 6.11)

Recalling the days in the Himalayas, Baba Lokenath often said, *"For more than a half century, my Gurudev took me through the most intense disciplines of yoga. With humble surrender I followed his instructions, traversing the diverse paths of yoga. If I ever had any doubt, he would guide me like the most patient and loving mother through the subtle problem to a higher experience. With deepest faith in him I easily moved along the path toward the goal. I passed through the most difficult stages of yoga practices only by his grace and able guidance. Drowned in the ocean of eternal bliss in the state of samadhi, I did not have any awareness of the time.*

"While in samadhi, heaps of snow would cover my body and would melt away. In that sublime state, I had no feeling of the existence of my body. I was in that state of samadhi (Cosmic Consciousness) for a long time. Finally, the effortless state of the Ultimate Truth was revealed. In that state

of consciousness, there was no separation between me and any other Cosmic manifestation. The inner and the outer all merged into each other as an expression of ultimate bliss, absolute joy. There is no state beyond this to be achieved in human life through total effort and Divine grace."

When Baba Lokenath merged into One Divine, the whole of nature celebrated. It takes a long time for Mother Nature to bring the Divine seed to full bloom. Baba was ninety years old. His Guru was a grand old man of one hundred and fifty years. However nature may have celebrated, there was one exception who did not, and that was Buddha Lokenath himself.

DISCIPLE AND GURU: A MIRROR OF LOVE

As Lokenath wept, he gazed up at the one who had led him to ultimate perfection. For the first time, he realized the true glory of his Guru. This great soul had not been concerned about his own liberation. He had sacrificed his life for the enlightenment of his disciples! Overwhelmed by this realization, Baba exclaimed, *"Oh, Gurudev! I have crossed the ocean of this Mayic (illusive) creation, only to find you still in the middle. You have withstood so much pain for me. As a result, I have been liberated, while you remain in the same state. I am not patient! I am concerned about when you will be freed."*

The state of no-mind, which the seeker experiences as Nirvikalpa samadhi, is a state beyond vibrations of good or bad, pure or impure, pain or pleasure, praise or insult, virtue or vice. Those who practice intense austerities for the sake of their own salvation do not return to body consciousness once they reach ultimate union.

For those with the seeds of compassion and love in their hearts, all dormant seeds of desire and tendencies dissolve and disappear in the state of no-mind. Only love and compassion remain. Jagad Guru, the Lord of the Universe, ordains these embodiments of love and compassion to redeem suffering humanity. The seeds of sexual energy are transformed into all encompassing, overflowing love. The instinct of anger transmutes into the sanctifying Divine energy of Compassion. The Lord manifests this transformation in the Satguru's Divinized body only to prove the unique and ultimate possibility of the human soul to the world. As Meister Eckhart says, "The seed of God is in us. Given an intelligent and hard working farmer, it will thrive and grow up to God, whose seed it is, and accordingly its fruits will be God-natured. Pear seeds grow into pear trees, nut seeds into nut trees, God-seed into God."

Guru Bhagwan had identified the excellent farmer in Lokenath. By nurturing the God-seed that flowered into the enlightened Lokenath, he knew that when Lokenath attained the Ultimate, great rivers of love and compassion would flow in every direction to sustain and transform the physical and spiritual lives of many. In the success of his disciple, Guru Bhagwan could foresee the emancipation and redemption of millions of suffering souls all over the world for ages to come. That was his greatest fulfillment as Guru. What more could the Guru desire or expect? That is why Guru Bhagwan worked so hard through his life for Lokenath. He felt privileged that his selfless efforts could bring those blessings to the world.

With motherly love, Guru Bhagwan lifted and embraced the tall, naked body of Lokenath, with its long, matted hair and every cell vibrating with Divine energy. In the Guru's eyes, Lokenath remained the small child of eleven years old who took his hand and started out from the village on the day of the sacred thread ceremony. He said to Lokenath, "Don't cry. Your unparalleled success has opened my eyes. I could see in you the practical demonstration of attainment from blending the paths of Jnana (discriminating knowledge) and Bhakti (devotional surrender) which Lord Krishna taught in the Gita. Seeking the Ultimate through discriminating intelligence is a dry path. I could forge in you the grandest combination of head and heart. You could reach the pinnacle only because you had such innocent surrender to your Guru and deepest faith in yourself and in God. Don't worry about me. We will soon go to Varanasi. There, I shall give up this old, worn out body and come in my next incarnation to you. Then it will be your responsibility to recognize me and put me on the path of this grand synthesis of yoga from the beginning. Make sure I don't commit the mistake again. Through you, the doors of eternal freedom will open to me."

Lokenath was delighted to hear his Guru's instruction. This was the opportunity for him to repay the rich debt he owed his Guru. All through his spiritual journey he had only received the loving care and service of his Guru. He could never offer anything back. He fell again at the feet of his Gurudev and praised him, saying, *"I am yours and I shall remain yours. You will work out your own liberation through this body of your disciple. I will be too happy to serve you any way you want."*

According to the scriptures, the Guru cannot surrender at the feet of the disciple while existing in the same body. The Guru, whether enlightened or not, is the Guru, the embodiment of Existence-Consciousness-Bliss Absolute. For the disciple either to disobey the Guru or to grant spiritual shelter to the Guru would not be in keeping with the spiritual guidelines set forth in the ancient Vedic scriptures — even if the disciple, as in the case of Baba Lokenath, is Yoga-Siddha, the Awakened One. Therefore, Guru Bhagwan had to return in the next life if he wished to receive enlightenment from Lokenath. Guru Bhagwan could have easily attained that state in the same life under the guidance of another Guru if he had wished to do so. Both Guru Bhagwan and Lokenath honored the authority of the scriptural injunctions which required Guru Bhagwan to come back with a new body and attain Self-Realization. This is an episode unique in spiritual history.

There is no bond stronger or more incomprehensible than the bond between the Guru and disciple. The relationship may change throughout many lifetimes, but the bond which is forged in the fires of the soul can never be broken. The Guru and disciple will always recognize each other. Thus, Guru Bhagwan knew that he would find Lokenath in his next life.

This episode in the Divine life of Lokenath teaches us a silent lesson. Even if the Guru is unenlightened, by the grace of God working through the Guru, the faithful disciple -- who practices the path shown by the Guru with unquestioning dedication -- can attain Self-Realization. As the disciple benefits from the Guru's Self-Realization, the Guru is also showered with unlimited grace through the pure vehicle of the enlightened disciple. The Guru is 'One Without the Second,' the Lord of the Universe.

MEDITATION

Though the enlightenment achieved by Baba is beyond our comprehension, by virtue of His Oneness with all Creation, Baba is within us. We can open ourselves to receive infusions of his exalted energy.

Take a few moments to open your heart to Baba at an energy level. Ask Baba to feed your heart and soul with the energy of his Cosmic Consciousness in ways which you can absorb and experience that are beyond words. Feel his presence vibrating within you.

Then prayerfully re-read Baba's descriptions of his enlightened state. Feel his Divine energy flowing through the conduits of his words into your body in ways that are beyond knowing. Close your eyes to more fully absorb any stirrings of energy, grace, insight, or connection to Baba that occur in the course of the reading.

Repeat this meditation often.

CHAPTER 6

A UNIFYING BRIDGE BETWEEN RELIGIONS

AFTER BABA LOKENATH attained enlightenment, the three yogis left their Himalayan caves and proceeded to Mecca and Medina, the sacred Islamic pilgrimage sites. Having lived in the snowy peaks of the Himalayas for fifty years and mastered and synthesized the paths of his native Hindu tradition, Lokenath now set out with Guru Bhagwan and Benimadhav, determined to study the Holy Koran.

They walked the entire distance from the Himalayas to Kabul. The Muslims, seeing the radiant energies of the three yogis, welcomed them. Mollasadi, a great scholar of the Holy Koran, came forward to greet them. He invited them to his home to be his honored guests, where they stayed and studied the Koran under his guidance.

Baba Lokenath made his own body a laboratory of the eternal Truth that, while paths may be many, the goal is One and shared by all religions. Through his study of the Koran, Baba undertook a second journey to the same One Truth which he had already attained through the practice of yoga.

In the Bhagavad Gita, Lord Krishna says that whatever the holy ones do, the larger masses must follow. Baba was enacting, for all humanity, the path we must take. As a living example, Baba demonstrates the Universal Spirit which is the essence of all true spiritual experience. Baba points us toward the peace and harmony which all religion is about. Baba asks us to look to the higher realms, to the direct experience of the Divine, where all barriers and all divisions between religions disappear. He calls us to forget the differences at the lower levels of belief, form and ritual. It is only through ignorance of deeper truths and identification with external forms of ritual that fanatics and fundamentalists fight to prove their religion over others. Without their own true religious experience, the masses become sheep who are easily manipulated into following the interpretations of teachers who are also without deeper experience. The all-too-frequently divisive and destructive history of interaction between the world religions is perpetuated in a cycle of ignorance about the true nature of the Divine. God is One, Oneness itself, inclusiveness itself, seeking the genuinely opened heart.

Baba wanted to facilitate better understanding of the essential harmony that existed between Hinduism and Islam. Through understanding, followers of both religions would no longer be bound by the ignorance that caused them to engage in religious violence over superficial differences arising from external rituals and practices.

In the world of the Enlightened One, there is no such thing as discrimination because everything is manifestation of the One. Baba Lokenath wanted to prove that all rivers ultimately merge into the one ocean, that all religions are the means to reach the final realization of the All Pervading Paramatman. After attaining Siddhi through the practice of all spiritual disciplines prescribed by the Vedic scriptures, he chose to demonstrate that the same truth could be realized through the faith of Islam. His study and practice of the principles of the Koran, and his bold statement, *"I am a Mussalman,"* were intended to bridge the widening gap between the people of these two faiths.

Baba wanted to give loving shelter to his Hindu devotees and also to embrace the children of Islam as his own. His universal love embraced all religions and all faiths. Baba had become the sea of Divine Grace, and people belonging to all faiths came to drink his compassionate love. Muslim devotees, who considered him a Pir, a Realized One, would bring their newborn babies and children to Baba's ashram to receive his blessings. The door of the ashram was open to all, regardless of caste or creed. Baba poured his abundant blessings continuously upon whoever came. Like Jesus, by the power of his example, Baba Lokenath teaches us to extend the boundaries of our compassion and love to include all.

THE AUTHOR'S EXPERIENCE AT BARADI

It seems appropriate to share my personal experience when visiting Baradi, 35 kilometers from Dacca, in 1994.

Today, the ashram remains a pilgrimage site for both Hindus and Muslims. On auspicious occasions like Baba's mahasamadhi celebrations, millions of people visit the ashram.

When I arrived, I was deeply touched to see a large number of Muslim brothers sitting in the ashram under the old mango trees, with their Hindu brothers beside them. An old Muslim man came forward to welcome me with tears in his eyes. He embraced me, trembling with ecstasy.

That night, a young Muslim man of 30 came to me and said, "In this ashram, Baba is very much alive. We can feel his divine energy. No Muslim can ever destroy this temple of Baba. Here, no violence or evil energy will work. For Baba is supreme here." He said, "I told my mother, 'When you die, I will take the dust of this ashram of Baba and put it in your grave and you will rest in eternal peace by the grace of Baba.'"

I woke up early the next morning after a couple of hours of the most peaceful sleep of my life. I saw many Muslim women in black robes, with their faces covered, coming to the ashram with lit candles and offerings to Baba. They have such deep faith in Baba, that whatever they want from Baba is granted.

In the evening, at the Arati (a devotional offering of a lighted oil lamp at the altar) to Baba in the temple, I was invited to sing and speak about the glory of Satguru Lokenath. I was filled with ecstasy to see such a large gathering of Hindu and Muslim brothers and sisters in the same place, sharing the vibrations of Universal Unity.

A visit to Baradi is the transforming experience of a lifetime. The presence of this Compassionate Buddha, who lived there continuously for 26 years, has energized each particle of dust to a high level of spiritual power. Thousands of people pour in every day, getting their wishes fulfilled by the powerful Presence of Baba Lokenath. The doors of this universal temple to living Divinity are open to the whole of humankind, without any barriers, religious or otherwise — not only for the fulfillment of mundane desires, but to give seekers entrance to the Higher life of their Spirit. The intensity of Baba's Presence spontaneously awakens seekers who come to the true purpose of our human birth, while opening the way to attain it.

On his way from Mecca to Medina through the desert, Lokenath met a yogi of very high attainment. Abdul Gaffar, as he was popularly known, was four hundred years old. Although he primarily remained silent, the spiritual attainment and powers of this yogi were known to all.

When Lokenath took his seat before him, Abdul Gaffar asked Lokenath, "Who are you?" Lokenath replied, *"I have come to you to learn who I am."*

Pleased with this reply, the yogi took Lokenath in his arms and hugged him. Abdul Gaffar asked him again, "How many days old are you?"

Lokenath paused for a moment, deeply contemplating the significance of the question. Understanding that the yogi was inquiring about his memory of previous incarnations, Lokenath replied, *"I am of two days,"* indicating that he could remember all about his two previous incarnations. Abdul Gaffar said, "I am of four days. I remember the experiences of my last four incarnations."

The two seers of Truth shared their individual experiences of the highest spiritual plane with each other. The meeting was a historic one. In the course of his talks with Lokenath, Abdul Gaffar expressed his respect for Guru Bhagwan, saying, "You have reached such a high state only through the grace and able guidance of your Guru. I did not get the guidance of such a competent master in my life."

In later years at Baradi, Baba Lokenath taught the world about the universality of all religions. The subtle way in which he chose to impart his wisdom is difficult to understand. He surprised his devotees by calling himself a 'Mussalman' (Muslim), though he was a Hindu by birth. Asked why he had called himself a Mussalman, Baba said, *"The word Mussalman is derived from 'Mussalam Imaan,' which means one in whom there is total Divinity."* In the same spirit of universality, Baba said, *"I have traveled extensively all over the world and have found only three Brahmins: Abdul Gaffar, Trailangya Swami and myself."* A Brahmin according to Baba is the Knower of Brahman, the Supreme Truth, rather than a person born into a family of the traditional Brahmin caste. Though Abdul Gaffar was Muslim by faith, he was a Brahmin in the purest sense as the Knower of Brahman, Absolute Reality.

Baba's statement, *"I am Mussalman,"* and his reference to Abdul Gaffar as a Brahmin have deep spiritual significance. He made these bold and controversial statements when religious dogmatism was at a peak to establish that an individual can reach beyond human limitations by sincere spiritual practice, despite conditioning imposed by sects of Hinduism, Islam, and Christianity.

After leaving Mecca, Guru Bhagwan decided that the time had come to give up his old, worn out body. As the day approached, he told Lokenath and Benimadhav that he wished to proceed to Kashi (Varanasi), the holy pilgrimage site on the bank of the Mother Ganges.

On their way to Varanasi, they met a great yogi called Hithlal Mishra, who was popularly known in Varanasi as Trailangya Swami, the Living Shiva. He lived for more than two hundred and fifty years and could recollect the experiences of his last three births.

Guru Bhagwan was relieved to meet Trailangya Swami because he had been worried about the care of his young children. Over the decades, he had developed the tender love of a mother toward Lokenath and Benimadhav. He could not think of them as more than his children, though they were a hundred years old at the time. He felt confident that Trailangya Swami was the right person to assume the responsibility for their care. One day he placed the hands of both Lokenath and Benimadhav into the hands of Hithlal. With tears in his eyes, he said, "Today, I have placed the responsibility of these two young boys of mine into your able hands. From this day forward, you will be their guardian." Trailangya Swami agreed in silence.

Soon after this, Guru Bhagwan went to Manikarnika Ghat on the bank of the holy Ganges and left his physical body while sitting in meditation. Lokenath knew that his beloved Gurudev was no more, so he gently touched the body and it fell to the ground. As the most devoted son and disciple, Baba Lokenath performed the last ceremonial rites, observing all the prescribed spiritual injunctions.

Thus passed Guru Bhagwan Ganguly. He was an illustrious son of Mother India who had dedicated his entire life to the making of a Godman, who was in turn destined to shelter the world like a mighty Banyan tree. As he lost himself in service in this life, Guru Bhagwan would be rewarded with his own Realization in the next, as Baba Lokenath had promised.

MEDITATION

Visualize the earth from space: a gleaming blue and green jewel that sparkles with Divinity in all of its life forms. See the peoples of each continent throughout time, touched by the sacred all around them, honoring the Divine through their own cultural spiritual traditions.

Visualize the life of light that has always flowed through the prayers of every human heart. Each day, that light has encircled the globe, flowing from the souls of the greatest saints and the simplest people. See every act of kindness, every unselfish act, every effort to lift life beyond limitation and circumstance, as a prayer of pure light. Experience the beauty of that light...its shimmering sweetness...its capacity to strengthen and encourage the good in every other heart. See the planet and its people healed as all humanity comes to claim the magnitude of this light as our true human heritage. See that light joyfully dancing and singing through all our lives, bringing us home to our Oneness in the Divine.

CHAPTER 7

BABA WALKS THE EARTH

After Guru Bhagwan's passing, Lokenath had a deep urge to explore the farthest reaches of the earth. He had inwardly seen much of the world and all that is beyond its materiality within the exalted states of his own pure and unified consciousness. He now chose to walk the earth, to personally and physically attend, as rarified Divine witness, to the earth's endless array of sublime manifestations of the Divine essence.

The Vedas proclaim the highest insight possible for humankind to be, "Sarvam khalu edam brahman" (All is verily the Brahman, pure consciousness). It is this pure energy of Divine Consciousness which is the source of all being and form. As the primal, creative, elemental Divine Essence, it pours itself into ever-new forms of manifestation. This immanent Divine within is the One whose existence shines through the many. All we need is the eyes and heart to see.

To ordinary human consciousness, the world we see and touch, taste and smell is factual and concrete. It gives convincing, millennia-reinforced evidence of separate, material realities. This habitual mode of perception fetters the human mind and blinds us to the subtler, ultimate truth of our own Divine Source and being. We are all subject to the dance of illusion, Maya, in a world in which the One is in a constant state of flux and change. We are prisoners, shut out from the dazzling, multi-dimensional reality of our own life and the extent of its participation in the larger life around us. Only the Self-Realized Vedantin sees consistently with integral sight, delighting in both the play of Maya and the full revelation of the Divinity it obscures. Beyond that, as 'One Without the Second', the Non-Dual Self sees, as its very own being, the full brilliance of luminous reality dancing through all manifestation. In that state of Oneness, in the state of "I am," "All that is, is S/He."

Baba Lokenath spoke little about his extensive travels, but what little he did reveal is extraordinary. The great yogis, Lokenath, Benihmadhav and Trailangya Swami traveled together for thirty to forty years. They started on foot to see the western world first. Regarding this part of the journey, Baba said very little except for a brief remark, that, *"The limit of travel to the west was the sea."* Once, a few English people visited Baba's ashram at Baradi and were discussing an English word which is pronounced differently by the French. Baba spoke a few words of French and told them that he had visited France. Therefore, we can at least assume that he toured the European continent to the Atlantic Ocean.

Trailangya Swami

Altogether, Baba made three visits to Mecca and Medina during his lifetime, traveling on foot. In Mecca, he was highly respected by the Muslims and was considered to be a saint of great attainment and spiritual power. He was always treated with utmost hospitality. In the words of Baba, *"The Muslims told me, 'If you want to cook for yourself, you are most welcome to do so. We will supply you with all the food you need. If you allow us, we will most gladly cook for you.' I agreed to the second proposition. They observed all the rituals of cleanliness and covered their mouths while preparing the meals so that the food would not become contaminated with the saliva that might fall from the tongue while talking."*

When the three yogis came to Medina, a large number of people were naturally drawn to Lokenath by his strong spiritual presence and by his mastery and knowledge of the Koran. Islamic seekers came to him as a Realized Master, surrendering to his spiritual guidance through their own path of Islam. It gratified and amazed them to see a Hindu yogi from the Himalayas who had such profound wisdom and command of the deepest secrets of Islam.

Local Islamic religious teachers visited him full of doubts about the real purpose of this Hindu. They were stunned to hear him giving the deepest and most natural interpretations possible of the Koran. Won over by his childlike innocence and the tenderness of his sublime love, which transcended all religious barriers, they gave Baba their love and support.

The people visiting Baba never went away empty-handed. Most Muslims came with homemade sweets, offering them at his feet. After tasting a little, Baba distributed them to the assembled seekers with his blessings. It was a rare thrill for the inhabitants of Mecca and Medina to meet yogis from India who were embodiments of pure love and universality.

After traveling extensively through Arabia, Israel, Persia, Afghanistan and various parts of Europe, the three returned to the loving lap of the mother Himalayas. Tired of traveling only on the plains, Lokenath decided to undertake the historic journey along the Mahaprasthana. This was the path through the Himalayan ranges described in the Mahabharata, which Yudhisthira traveled with the other the Pandava brothers and their wife, Draupadi, in order to reach heaven with their physical bodies after Sri Krishna left His body. Even today, beyond the Badrikasham Temple there is a path which is said to be the path to Mahaprasthana, meaning the final retreat.

Baba Lokenath wanted to travel the same route. However, before commencing the journey, he knew it was wise to first acclimatize their bodies to the freezing temperatures so that they could live and walk without difficulty. For this reason he and Benimadhav stayed in the Badrikashram area during both the cold as well as hot seasons. This area remains closed for six to eight months of the year, and it is humanly impossible to stay there all year around. Even today, the gates of the Holy Shrine of Badrinath Temple are closed for more than six months. During that time the entire temple is covered with snow.

Lokenath and Benimadhav lived in this area for three long years absolutely naked to grow accustomed to the severe climatic conditions. At the end of that time, Trailangya Swami appeared before them expressing his desire to walk with them to the Sumeru regions. Lokenath was more than happy to take him along, but he asked that Trailangya Swami accustom himself to living and walking in such a cold climate to avoid any unforeseen difficulties. The three yogis lived in the Badrikashram area for an additional three years to grow further accustomed to the freezing temperatures. Then they began their arduous journey and proceeded through the Himalayan peaks along the path of Mahaprasthana.

During the course of this long, tedious climb they occasionally ate some kandamul (wild roots). According to Baba, this was good enough.

Baba Lokenath told his disciple, Sri Brahmananda Bharati, *"We did not even have any warm clothing to cover our bodies. We were stark naked. By living and walking like this for a long time, a white layer of skin appeared on our bodies. It gave us natural protection against the freezing cold. Walking like this, we reached Manosarovar."* Those devotees of Baba who saw him during his initial days at Baradi had the unique opportunity to see this white layer of skin, which gradually disappeared while living on the plains at Baradi.

As Baba spoke about his travels, he mentioned Manosarovar. When asked whether he was referring to the Manosarovar of the Tibet region, Baba Lokenath said, *"Your Manosarovar is right at the corner of your house,"* indicating that it is very close. The Manosarovar Baba referred to is different from the one people often visit in Tibet, at the foot of the famous Kailash Mountain, which is considered by the Hindus as Lord Shiva Himself. Baba talked about Manosarovar, the great Lake in the Himalayan region unknown to travelers and pilgrims, and known only to mystics of high attainment.

From further details which Baba gave periodically to his disciples describing this odyssey, it was evident that the three yogis walked toward the north and crossed the borders of Siberia in eastern Russia. They walked further northward for thousands of miles and finally reached a place which he called *the 'Land of No-Sun',* the darkest region on this planet. Unable to see well enough to continue walking in those deep, dark areas, they decided that it would be best to remain where they were until they were able to continue safely.

Baba said, *"After we stayed there for some time our eyes naturally adjusted to the darkness. Our vision, as well as the shape of our eyes, became like those of a cat. We came to see in the same manner as one sees objects in flashes of lightning during a storm. Eventually, we developed the power to see even in the dark. And when we could see in that darkness, we advanced further."*

Baba also described other unbelievable experiences in these dark regions, saying, "*During our stay there, we saw some very unusual human beings of very short height, ranging from one foot to one and a half feet. Their bodies were white complexioned and they moved about naked in the icy polar region. At first, they were quite frightened when they saw our tall human stature. When they saw our peaceful attitude, they realized that we were harmless creatures. They collected kandamul (wild roots) for our food and would leave the roots near us, but they would never come close to us. We could not understand a bit of their language. But we observed them for a long time quite closely and could understand them by their behavior patterns. We discovered that there was no institution of marriage in their society. They moved about most freely. Although I could not understand their language, I could grasp certain words which they often used like 'ambian' and 'dhokar.'*"

The wandering yogis traveled through the 'Land of No-Sun' for a very long time. It was difficult for them to determine the passage of time since the sun did not rise or set. Apparently, they had to calculate the time on the basis of the snow piling up and melting. The former was accepted as the season of winter and the later as summer.

It took years to go to Sumeru and return. Sumeru is the holiest of all mountains according to Hindu Mythology. Lord Krishna says in Vibhuti Yoga that among all the mountains, He is Sumeru, signifying the sacredness of this mountain in the far north of the globe. A visit to this mountain, which is frequented by celestial beings, is considered holy according to Hindu myth.

When they returned to the plains, Trailangya Swami expressed a desire to proceed east, so all three continued in that direction. When they reached China, the border security guards caught sight of the unusual looking trio. They immediately arrested them and put them behind bars. But to their surprise, the captors discovered that in a spirit of absolute indifference, their captives were able to pass in and out of the prison through the locked gates. The king, realizing the great mystic powers of his prisoners, immediately set them free.

For a long time the three great yogis had traveled extensively together. Now it was time for Trailangya Swami to give directions to Baba Lokenath. When Baba indicated that he would like to accompany Trailagya Swami to the far east, Trailangya Swami said, "Lokenath, please do not come with me any further. You have a Divine mission to perform in the lower plains. Go ahead with your mission." The three parted company, with Mahayogi Trailangya Swami moving alone toward the east and Baba Lokenath and Benimadhav proceeding toward the Himalayas on the way to Tibet.

MEDITATION

Why did Baba walk the Earth? Was he blessing the world in some way, as a fully conscious witness to its beauty and goodness? Was he reinforcing its foundation before the onslaught of the 20th Century's destruction and desecration?

Visualize Baba bending over flowers, standing on glacial mountain tops, under trees, beside streams, watching and listening to birds, fascinated by the unique beauty of each animal and insect.

Ask Baba to enthrall and awaken you to the awareness of the Divine in all life. Ask him to show you new ways to walk and love the Earth. Pray for the capacity to become a deeper, fuller witness to the Divinity manifesting itself through Earth's richness and beauty. Spend more time outside, receiving the love, blessings and revelations of Earth's myriad, ecstatic energies. Become the Divine Child at play, in a universe of sheer delight.

CHAPTER 8

BABA COMES TO BARADI

LEAVING CHINA, LOKENATH and Benimadhav passed through the Tibetan borders to the foothills of the Himalayas. A long arduous walk over the Himalayan regions and the plains brought them to the hills of Chandranath in eastern India.

A fascinating incident occurred during their stay in this area. One day, Lokenath was sitting under a tree in the jungle. The wild roar of a tiger suddenly broke the silence. Sensing pain, Baba meditated on the source of the animal's trouble and soon realized that it was a tigress that had just given birth to several handsome cubs. She was extremely anxious about leaving the cubs unprotected in order to search for food and was roaring in helplessness and frustration. Feeling deep compassion for her, Baba Lokenath appeared before the frantic mother to assure her of his protection of the cubs. Relieved that she could leave the cubs in his care, she went in search of food.

A rare bond of love and trust was forged, with the tigress routinely leaving the cubs behind with Baba while she went hunting. After the cubs had grown a bit, Baba thought himself free of responsibility and started out again on his travels with Benimadhav. After going only a short distance, however, the tigress was roaring again. Baba knew it was a call from her. Understanding that the tigress did not feel the cubs were ready to be left on their own, Lokenath had no choice but to grant the prayer of the mother. He remained for a period of two to three more months until the cubs had grown enough to accompany their mother on her hunts.

As they were preparing to leave again, Benimadhav, Baba's trusted boyhood friend and spiritual companion, expressed a desire to visit the holy shrine of the Divine Mother at Kamakshya in Assam. The time to part had arrived. Lokenath gave his consent and promised he would always bless Benimhadhav with his subtle presence and help whenever and wherever Benimadhav called upon him. They said farewell and Benimadhav left for Kamakshya. Not much is authentically known about Benimadhav after this physical separation. Many devotees of various saints claimed that their Guru was Baba's companion Benimadhav, but there is no way to authenticate any of those claims.

Lokenath started toward the plains. Coming down from the hills and jungles of Chandranath, he encountered a terrible wildfire. While birds flew to safety, for most of the panic stricken animals, there was no escape. They were engulfed in raging flames.

One of the great saints of Bengal, Prabhupada Vijay Krishna Goswami, had been meditating under a tree when the fire broke out. Disturbed from meditation by the wild cries of the animals and birds, he looked up to discover himself in a circle of flames. Death seemed imminent, but he did not feel fear. With his heart utterly surrendered to the Divine, Vijay prayed for God's help. When he opened his eyes, he saw an extremely tall, totally naked and brilliant human figure approaching him through the flames. Vijay assumed it was a vision, but the luminous being with long matted locks lifted Vijay in his arms, placed him on his shoulder, and carried him effortlessly through the fire. When Vijay returned to his senses, he found himself lying in a safe place with no trace of his mysterious savior.

Years later, when Vijay Krishna Goswami met Baba at his Baradi ashram, Baba asked him who had saved him from the wildfire in the Chandranath hills. Vijay Krishna Goswami immediately recognized Baba and prostrated himself at Baba's feet. Vijay Krishna Goswami became Baba Lokenath's most ardent devotee. Vijay lavishly praised Baba and his spiritual powers and attainment, spreading the word of Baba wherever Goswami went. Though Vijay Krishna Goswami had a great mission of his own as a spiritual preceptor, it was through him that thousands of people throughout Bengal came to know about Baba Lokenath and began flooding to Baba's ashram at Baradi.

Vijay Krishna Goswami often told his devotees about how he came to discover Baba Lokenath at Baradi. It seems that during one of his pilgrimages to Manosarovar and the higher regions of the Himalayas, he had the rare opportunity to receive the darshan of several saints who were sitting in a deep meditative state in a Himalayan cave. Their bodies were very old. The yogis appeared to have been absorbed in penance for centuries. When Goswami prostrated himself at their feet, one of them opened his eyes. When Goswami prayed for his grace, the yogi said, "Why have you taken pains to come to these heights? A Mahapurusha, a yogi of much higher attainment than we are, is living right near your home."

At the time, Goswami was unaware of Baba Lokenath's presence at Baradi. When he came to Baba and received Baba's Divine

Grace, however, he remembered the words spoken to him by the yogi. He knew that this was the Mahapurusha about whom the yogi had spoken.

After rescuing Goswami, Baba walked down to the village of Daudkandi, in the district of Tripura. At that time, Dengu Karmakar, a native of Baradi, a village located in the Narayanganj district, (Bangladesh), was staying in Daudkandi due to a court case in which he was involved.

Dengu was beside himself due to the criminal charge he was facing. There seemed to be nothing he could do. He was certain that he would be proven guilty, a verdict that would most probably result in the death sentence. Dengu's lawyers had been exploiting him, continually demanding more money. In a desperate attempt to raise the needed funds, Dengu began going from door to door in search of loans. Suddenly, Dengu saw a naked sadhu sitting under a tree, staring at him with fixed eyes. The sadhu had a thin, frail body of considerable height. The moment Dengu saw the holy man, he felt peaceful and secure. Without any hesitancy, Dengu fell at Baba's feet, tearfully pouring his troubles out to the saint. Baba listened patiently. When Dengu had emptied himself, Baba spoke to him with a soft, affectionate voice.

> *"All your attempts to find loans are in vain. No one will lend you anything. You need not worry about all that anymore. Go straight to the court. I have written the judgment through the hands of the judge. You will be acquitted."*

Dengu ran to the court and found that the promise of the saint had come true. His joy knew no bounds. His heart was overflowing with gratitude and reverence for the unknown saint. Without wasting a moment at the courthouse, Dengu dashed back to the tree to find the saint sitting in the same posture. This time, Baba had a different expression on his face. He appeared to be absolutely indifferent, as though nothing had happened. Dengu fell at Baba's feet express to his deep gratitude while Baba sat motionless, lost in his own world.

As Dengu sat at Baba's feet, a sweet fragrance from Baba's body filled him with happiness. For the first time in his life, he felt relieved of all pain and tension. He was no longer concerned about his home, his properties, or his family. He was possessed only by the great being who sat before him. Baba seemed strangely familiar, but Dengu could not imagine where he might have met him.

After a long while, Baba looked at Dengu. With folded hands, Dengu said, "It is only through your grace that I have gotten back everything in life. But you are the greatest gift of all. You are God in human form. Now tell me where you live. If you wish, I can help you reach that place."

Baba smiled and answered, *"The whole world is my home. I have already reached home."* Dengu, a very simple man with little education and intelligence, barely understood Baba's words. Dengu thought that Baba had no residence of his own. So he caught hold of Baba's feet and begged Baba to stay with him at his small cottage in the village.

Baba tried to convince Dengu that his neighbors would criticize him if he allowed a naked sannyasin to live in his home with the other members of the family. But Dengu would not relent. He had become deeply attached to the savior of his life. Leaving him was simply unthinkable. He was prepared to face any consequence to remain by Baba's side.

Baba knew that Dengu was destined to have the privilege of taking him to Baradi for his Divine Play. So Baba responded, *"I will stay wherever you like and will remain there as long as you wish."* Dengu ran to the nearby riverbank and hired a boat to take Baba to Baradi. There, Baba found a place in the household of Dengu Karmakar.

After a few days passed, sharp criticism arose against Dengu for allowing a naked madman to stay in his house with other family members. The words of Baba had come true. Even Dengu's own family members started vehemently opposing poor Dengu's decision. Baba remained absolutely indifferent to all that was happening around him. Finally, the criticisms and insults became too much for Dengu to bear, for they were unfounded and directed against the deity of his heart. Young boys and girls pelted Baba with stones and taunted him at every opportunity. Dengu stayed closely by his side to protect him. But whenever he was away, attending to his personal chores, the torture of Baba's body continued. The situation reached its peak one day when Baba had to take shelter behind a wild bush.

Dengu, who could no longer endure watching Baba suffer such cruel treatment by the neighbors, expressed the pain it caused him. Baba consoled Dengu saying, *"Is it right on our part to find fault with these innocent children? They do not know what they are doing; so how can I find fault with them? I have hardly any blood in my body.* (Once when Baba had cut open a part of his lower limb to examine the nature of his blood a paste-like fluid oozed out.) *So their stones cannot do much harm. The wounds will heal within a couple of days.*

"If I cannot tolerate these little insults and physical pains, how am I to bear in my heart the pains and miseries of millions and millions of devotees who are to come under my shelter? My Guru taught me the technique of the tortoise. The tortoise draws both its head and limbs into its tough shell whenever it anticipates an external attack. I, too, have a tough shell over my body. Insulting words cannot penetrate my skin and stones cannot do me any harm. I remain ever unaffected by all these external interferences."

The incident and Baba's response to it is a practical manifestation of the Bhagavad Gita's teachings on the 'sthitaprajna,' the One who is established in Divine Consciousness:

> "The Enlightened One is not depressed by physical, mental or social suffering, nor is he elated by any pleasures of material nature. He is ever free from all sense of attachment, fear and anger." (Bhagavad Gita 2.58)

> "The realized one controls his senses by his own free will just as the tortoise draws in its neck and limbs and extends them whenever it wants."
> (Bhagavad Gita 2.58)

According to Baba Lokenath, the Gita is a scripture not just to be regularly read or chanted. It is to be practiced in life, to be lived. The aim of life is to become the Gita. Baba was 'The Living Gita.'

One of Baba's closest disciples, Narisababa, once complained that Baba cared too much for the people that came before him with materialistic demands and hypocritical behavior. The Living Gita compassionately replied, *"Oh, they are so unhappy in life, so helpless. That's the reason they come and shed tears before me. If they receive a little from me, they are so happy. That's the reason I cannot ask them to go. How do you expect these poor householders to have faith and devotion to God when they are subjected to so much misery and unhappiness in their day-to-day lives? When I see their painful state, I cannot remain indifferent. I know very well that I do nothing. If they think that I am the one who bestows all the boons, what do I lose?"*

Baba remained indifferent to the physical and mental abuse that was inflicted upon him and stayed with Dengu until the end of Dengu's life. Since Baba had not yet revealed himself, people could not comprehend the height of his attainment. They dismissed him as a naked madman. When the moment arrived for him to reveal his Divine state, he signaled the beginning of his Divine Play with a miracle.

One day, a few Brahmin priests were sitting together busily preparing the sacred thread for a ceremony. In the process, the threads became knotted. The Brahmins could not unravel the threads and a quarrel arose among them.

Baba Lokenath suddenly appeared to them and said, *"Why are you all quarreling with each other? Do you not know the technique of unknotting the threads? And strangely, you call yourselves Brahmins!"*

At first, the Brahmins reacted sharply to the naked man's comments and said, "We know well that with the utterance of the sacred

Gayatri Mantra, the knots of the sacred thread are loosened. These knots, however, seem to be too tight. We are not able to unravel them."

Baba said, *"I do not know what kind of Brahmins you all are. Well, while I am doing the Gayatri Japa, the two of you will pull the knotted threads from both ends and they will be straightened."*

The Brahmins had mixed feelings about Baba. They had regarded him as a mindless madman. Now they were stunned by the authority with which he spoke about the scriptures. They could not ignore the power that radiated through his words and presence. Feeling compelled to follow his instructions, the two Brahmins began pulling both ends of the thread. As they did so, Baba began chanting the Gayatri Maha Mantra in the purest Vedic way. Transcendental vibrations filled the air and within seconds the entire thread had straightened itself without a single knot.

The Brahmins then recognized Baba as a great yogi and immediately prostrated themselves at his feet, asking for forgiveness.

News of the incident and about Baba's spiritual power spread swiftly to villages near and far. People in large numbers began visiting Baradi to have the darshan of the great yogi.

It was at this time that Dengu Karmakar died. Dengu's family had enjoyed the protection and blessings of Baba while he lived with them. With Dengu gone, members of his family started objecting strongly to Baba's continued stay in their house. Baba replied in a very dispassionate tone, *"I am a sannyasin. I have no objection to leaving, but the consequences are not going to be good. That is my only worry."* In fact, Dengu's family did not realize that the rise in their fortune was due to the presence of Baba, who is Laxmi (the Hindu Goddess of Wealth) Herself.

A family by the name of Nag was the richest among the landlords of Baradi at that time. The family had become deeply attached to Baba and always longed to serve Baba in whatever way he wished. When Baba left the home of Dengu Karmakar, they asked Baba if he would permit them to construct a permanent ashram for him. Baba accepted their offer, provided the ashram was constructed on land that was not taxed.

At the east of Baradi market, land was found which was untaxed because it had been formerly used to cremate the dead. Baba approved the property and the ashram, modeled after the ancient hermitage of the rishis, was constructed shortly thereafter.

When the ashram was completed, the Nag family requested that Baba clothe himself. After living almost one hundred and forty years as a naked sadhu, Baba Lokenath, in his usual state of indifference, placed the sacred thread around his neck and clothed his Divine body with a piece of white cloth. He then took his seat at the ashram and began dispensing his limitless treasures to the world.

MEDITATION

In making himself completely available to the tigress and to Dengu, Baba shows us how utterly available he is to every level of our need. The Divine wants all of us. The Godman asks us to bring all the large and small issues of every day life to our relationship with Him.

Resolve in the morning to be aware of Baba's loving presence in your heart throughout the day. Notice the ongoing stream of your daily concerns as you move through the day. Offer them all, in each moment, into his tender care. Ask him for advice as you would your dearest friend. Notice how simply answers form in your heart to your questions. Ask him for help on the smallest, most trivial issues. Share laughs, observations, moments of beauty — every aspect of your day — with him.

At the end of the day, take a moment to reflect back on the quality of your day and the difference it made to include Baba in all of it. Express your gratitude for the large and small graces he has sent your way.

CHAPTER 9

THE POWER OF FORGIVENESS

FOR MORE THAN twenty-six years, the lila that Baba Lokenath performed at his ashram at Baradi was recorded by his closest disciples. These accounts inspire us to the highest ideals of human life. While the facts and the anecdotes may be similar, the Master reveals the essence of the Divine Play differently to each devotee. When he radiates his light, one devotee may express it by singing his glory, while another may be inspired to write his message of inspiration and truth. But Baba is always the source of the inspiration and transformation.

Narisababa, who became one of Baba's most cherished disciples, did not begin with a flawless character. Before meeting Baba, he had been a person of little integrity who cloaked himself in the orange robes of renunciation.

In his early childhood days, Narisababa met a naked monk of questionable character who taught him to deceive. Learning the art of deception at an early age, Narisababa easily convinced unsuspecting villagers that he was a renounced monk. When he reached maturity, he left the company of his guru, confident that he, too, could play that role. As a guru, he attracted a few undesirable characters who became his associates and disciples. Moving from village to village with mules loaded with narcotics such as opium and hashish, he indulged in a life of sensual pleasure. At night his disciples would make arrangements so that he could satisfy the demands of his lower nature. This unrestrained life of the senses continued unchecked while Narisababa exploited innocent villagers in the name of God.

One day, after smearing his body with ashes, Narisababa sat under a tree next to an open fire. Suddenly he heard a powerful voice behind him, calling his old household name. He had never heard such a commanding voice in his life and was mystified. Turning around, Narisababa was stunned to find an extremely tall, naked yogi standing there. A strange feeling swept through Narisababa's body as he beheld the radiant being and felt Baba's piercing gaze. The Divine look penetrated Narisababa's heart, cleansing the impurities that had accumulated through many births. As if drawn by a powerful magnet, he fell at the feet of the yogi in absolute surrender.

Like a loving mother pardoning the transgressions of her child, Baba embraced Narisababa with tender affection, saying, *"You need not worry about your sins. They are all mine. From now on all your responsibilities are mine."*

That this kind of compassion and forgiveness was possible in another human being was beyond Narisababa's comprehension. Baba knew all of his past sins. When, with full knowledge, Baba took the responsibility of being his Guru, Narisababa was astonished and overwhelmed with gratitude. To remain away from the holy company of this saint even for a moment became unimaginable.

Having experienced one transforming look from Baba that changed the entire course of his life, Narisababa embraced Baba's

Divinity with abandon. He had never seen God face to face. Yet, all the qualities and ideals of all that he had insincerely preached were perfectly expressed in every aspect of Baba Lokenath. Baba had rescued Narisababa from a life of error and transformed him into an ardent devotee.

Narisababa was enchanted by the way Baba expressed himself when he taught. When he spoke, for instance, on the subject of Karma Yoga as outlined in the Bhagavad Gita, he spoke with the authority of one who had become God. Baba's words sang with Divine Energy. To listen to him was to sit at the source of the Divine Presence and to become absorbed in the living Heart of Truth.

Like Lokenath in his younger days, Narisababa wanted to learn the shastras. The all-knowing Baba told his disciple, *"My Guru did not allow me to take the path of acquiring knowledge from books. For you, too, I find no need for that.*

"To know yourself, first hear the Truth directly from your Guru, who is the living embodiment of the scriptures. With utmost trust in his words and devotion to him, practice the disciplines with all your might, without the slightest reservation.

"When you have emptied yourself in the process, you will realize that you are fulfilled, that you have flowered.

"The Gita is not reading material to be read as matter of routine. You must become the Gita. That is the entire purpose of the Gita.

"It is only through Divine Grace that you find the highest principles of love and surrender manifesting in the heart of the devotee. If you spend

your time in abstract discussions based on commentaries by various scholars, when will you dive deep and realize the truth and become the Gita?"

Once Narisababa asked Baba, *"Could you explain more about the concept of detached action and its practicality in day-to-day life?"*

Baba answered at length, *"Do you think all can follow the path of Nishkama Karma Yoga? Those who lead a worldly life of material desires face its adverse consequences until they realize that no material happiness is free of pain and sorrow. Eventually, their inner awareness increases. Gradually the importance of not being attached to the fruits of action dawns on them. The Gita spontaneously manifests in the hearts of such devotees. They become conscious and aware of the unhappiness that follows all material cravings. The path of Nishkama Karma Yoga opens of its own accord.*

"The devotee develops an ingrained trust in the Lord as the all-merciful and benevolent Presence. The mind of the devotee does not so easily and unconsciously chase after the fruits of action. The devotee realizes that the Beloved will grant whatever is begged for and then quickly withdraw, leaving the devotee to enjoy only the fruit. The true devotee does not feel at ease in the absence of the Divine. All action is performed with the mind fixed on the Divine, in constant prayer. The devotee constantly prays for detachment from the fruit of action and to be forever trained on the Lotus Feet of the Master.

"In the life of such a devotee, unhappiness and sorrows do come, but feeling the presence of God within and without as the sole protector, the mind remains unperturbed. With Him, whatever you do turns into a blissful experience."

Baba Lokenath continued, *"The Gita is not merely a book to be read. It is a song, a melody. No music lover reads music instead of listening to it. The rhythm, the harmony, the sweetness of the music cannot be directly experienced or enjoyed through reading! From time immemorial, the Eternal Lord has been sitting in the hearts of devotees. In the hearts of all living beings, he has been singing the Divine song. Who is conscious of it? The mind is always busy, thinking about the past, weaving dreams of the future, or being disturbed by the diverse array of sounds of the external world. The Divine Song is never heard. But the Divine does not stop singing. It will be singing until you hear."*

On another occasion, Narisababa asked Baba, "Our minds are restless. How are we to listen to this Divine Song from within?"

Baba replied, *"Without Divine Grace, nothing is possible. With Divine Grace, even the impossible becomes possible. When you receive Grace, your mind will spontaneously turn to the Divine. Then you will realize what the Gita is.*

"Surrender, unconditional surrender, is the path. You have to constantly try to surrender your ego, your mind and intellect to the Divine. This cannot be achieved in one day. All your miseries will come to an end the moment Divine Grace descends. For that moment to occur, you must first prepare yourself with devotion and the utmost perseverance.

"Look at the children around you? How innocent and simple they are. How natural their surrender to the mother is. There is no hypocrisy, no false pride of learning or wealth in them. With just one innocent demand, the mother happily responds to her child. Surrender yourself with the same simplicity and trust to the Divine. Surrender yourself to the

Supreme Authority of the Divine who loves you. Your prayers should be as simple and as pure as a child's. Demand whatever you want from your Divine parents. The Divine is the womb of your becoming, your Father and your Mother, the One who is most dear. The Divine is dearer than anyone in this world, the only One who can be totally trusted, the only One on whom you can exert all of your rights. As this awareness grows in your inner being, you will realize that you have grown closer to the Beloved. Your Beloved is no longer far away, but the Beloved One who sits in your own heart.

"The essence of yoga lies in your feeling for the Divine. The deeper the feeling, the more you are brought to a state of Oneness with the Beloved, who gradually manifests in your heart as the Sole Doer of all your activities. Then you will realize that you have become the living Gita. Karma, Bhakti and Jnana will find a harmonious blending in a synthesis of Supreme Perfection in you. Then, and then alone, will you realize why you have come into the world with this human body, and not before that."

On renunciation as set forth in the Gita, Baba says, "*True renunciation comes through acceptance of all that life offers. Detachment comes only through love for the Divine. The more the devotee loves the Divine with all his heart, the more evident the sense of detachment from transitory material things of life becomes.*

"Give your mind to the Guru. Think about His Glory. Meditate upon the supreme ideals of love and compassion which the Guru personifies. You will see that the Guru will allow you to enjoy life blissful. That which is to be rejected will leave you on its own accord for good. Instead of glorifying your ego, glorify Guru. Instead of suffering with the false vanity of being the doer, realize God and Guru as the only Doer.

"Divine Grace has such a natural transforming influence that the devotee need not renounce anything forcibly. People seeing the external manifestations of renunciation think about the greatness of the devotee. To the true devotee of the Lord, however, love and devotion are all important. Immersed in love, the true devotee is always flooded with Divine ecstasy, and material trifles lose their power and significance.

"At the root of all desires is God alone. Desiring and non-desiring are all part of the Divine Play. In the whole of Cosmic Creation, there is none but God."

Baba Lokenath's presence at the small ashram at Baradi became a source of fulfillment of the desires of all men and women who came there. Like the Kalpataru, the Wish-Fulfilling Tree of Hindu mythology, Baba showered the gifts of his grace without the slightest sense of discrimination.

Narisababa sometimes objected to Baba's indiscriminate attitude in granting all these wishes. Baba would lovingly respond, *"You judge people only by their external form or by the words they speak, because your eyes cannot see beyond the material skin. But I see the One alone in everybody, pure and perfect. Whatever I see appears to be pure and perfect.*

"Good, bad, virtue or vice, all these are relativities of a relative world, the creation of material mind. I belong to a world where there is no discrimination. Everything is beautiful. I am in this world of yours, but on the day, long ago, that I realized who I am, I lost the capacity to think as all of you do. I cannot find fault with anyone. Whatever I see, good or bad, it is all Divine.

"Whenever people come to me with depressed hearts, full of misery and anguish, I see the Beloved in them. I lose myself, entranced with the Divine I see. In the meantime, the Lord fulfills the desires of the devotees. The devotees see me and think of me as the doer, but I know that He alone is the Doer, the One bestowing all mercy and grace."

Narisababa related an incident which reveals, once again, the depth of Baba's compassion and Divine Perfection.

One day a newly married couple visited the ashram. The young bride was pale and appeared to be seriously depressed. It seemed as though something had been troubling her for a long period of time. After the newlyweds prostrated themselves before Baba, the husband excused himself and left the room.

Alone, in the Divine Presence of Baba, the woman felt inexpressible feeling of peace and serenity. She longed to empty herself of the problems which had burdened her, but she was too ashamed to confess her misdeeds or to speak to Baba about the painful memory of her sins. With tearful and repentant, downcast eyes, she waited for Baba to break the intolerable silence.

The compassionate mother in Baba spoke to her, *"Why are you suffering so much? What sins have you committed? You need not tell them to me; I know everything about your past and I knowingly ask why you are unnecessarily causing yourself pain by thinking yourself a sinner?*

"Whatever you have done, have you done it all by your own will? How little you know of yourself. You think and wish to do many things, but are you always successful in doing them according to your will? If

your will is so helpless against the invisible will that directs you from within, then why are you thinking that you are the sinner?"

Although the young woman did not understand Baba's words, her mind became tranquil. She felt the Divine Presence within her heart.

The woman said, "Baba, I am not able to pardon myself for all my evil doings. The faith and love that my husband has for me adds to the fire of my inner agony which I can neither express nor endure. Sometimes I feel that I should commit suicide to end this agonizing state in my life."

Baba, the Divine physician, consoled the unhappy woman, *"Have you ever thought about who it is that motivates you from within to do right or wrong? I am the One sitting in the very core of your heart. It is my will alone which plays through you. If the will is mine, then how can the sin be yours? If anybody is to be blamed it is not you, but me."*

The young woman was incredulous. She had never before heard anything like this. The Godman who was smiling so compassionately not only exonerated her, but also assumed the blame for the sins that she had committed.

Baba said, *"You will not understand my words, but always keep in mind that you are not a sinner anymore. Your husband is a nice boy and he has no complaints against you. He only wants you to be happy in life. From today, I take total responsibility for you both. Leave all the thoughts of sin and your past with me and go back home to lead a happy married life. You will see that you will have no more troubles in life."*

The woman felt as if she had been touched by magic. The heaviness of her heart and mind dissolved, leaving no trace of her past agony. She was at peace. Bathed in the Divine Grace of Baba, she surrendered at his feet saying, *"Baba, you have showered me with so much grace. Bless me, so that I may always remember your kindness and grace by remaining ever engaged in devotional service to your Lotus Feet."*

From his state of Supreme Divinity, Baba declared, *"The One is everywhere. There is no second. Who will show kindness to whom? Have you ever seen a person in this world who is kind to him self? I do not find the existence of anything other than Me in this entire creation. I have traveled in the hills and mountains, in the jungles and forests, all over the world, but could only see Myself. You will not understand why I love you all so much, why I am sharing your miseries and unhappiness."*

The husband and wife drank the nectar of Baba's eternal words. Prostrating themselves at the feet of this living embodiment of love and compassion, they took their leave of Baba with his words still ringing in the young woman's ears.

MEDITATION

Put on some exquisite music or find a beautiful spot in nature in which to spend some time writing and praying. Write about the things that you feel most guilty about, now or in the past. Go deep. Be truthful with yourself and with God. Then imagine yourself at the high altar of Baba, the Divine, or of your Guru, if you have one. Offer all of your guilt, all sense of shame and fault and sin, into the loving heart of the Divine. Lay your burdens down, and leave them, at the loving Lotus Feet of the Divine altar. Experience being fully forgiven. Rest in the tender light of God's compassion, for as long as possible. Pray or meditate, asking the Divine for the ability to walk confidently in the flowing light of grace. Then find a way to express your gratitude to God and to Life.

CHAPTER 10

VIJAY KRISHNA SEES BABA'S COSMIC FORM

GOSWAMI'S FIRST MEETING WITH BABA

WHEN THE SEED of Divinity comes to full blossom in an individual, the fragrance of the Divine flower so permeates the atmosphere that creatures are drawn from near and far. So it was with Baba that people found their way to his ashram.

While living with Dengu Karmakar, Baba had disguised himself as a mad beggar. He cheerfully withstood the insults and abuses from the villagers without the slightest retaliation. When the time was ripe, he revealed himself by manifesting his supernatural powers.

After the miracle of the sacred thread, the ashram at Baradi became a holy pilgrimage center. Regardless of caste, color or creed, people flocked to the ashram to pay their respects to Baba, to have his darshan, to receive his blessings, and to fulfill their myriad personal desires through his grace.

As is most often the case, the priceless gift of Truth was rarely requested, so Baba listened patiently to the mundane problems of ordinary householders. People with terrible diseases came in large numbers. Collapsing at the feet of Baba, they begged for his mercy. Baba's grace and compassion would flow out to them like the holy water of the Mother Ganges, purifying their hearts and curing of their physical ailments. No one returned from Baba's ashram unfulfilled.

In December, 1887, Prabhupada Sri Vijay Krishna Goswami, a Guru of great stature, came to meet Baba at Baradi after an extended pilgrimage to the sacred sites of India.

Baba was sitting in his cottage with a few devotees. He suddenly said, *"Vijay is coming. His boat has gotten stuck in the sand of the riverbank near Chamarbari," and* asked a few devotees to go greet Vijay and bring him to the ashram.

When Baba's devotees reached the riverbank, they found the boat stuck in the sand and inquired whether Vijay Krishna Goswami had come. The astonished devotees of Vijay Krishna asked how they knew of his arrival. Baba's devotees told them that Baba Lokenath had instructed them to go to the riverbank to meet Goswami and escort him back to the ashram.

Vijay Krishna Goswami entered the ashram and stood in the doorway of the room where Baba was sitting in his usual Gomukhasana posture. In a spontaneous meditative trance, Goswami saw Baba in His Cosmic Form, and began proclaiming, "Oh! He is the Self-Illumined One! The light of the sun is radiating from his body. I see gods and goddesses all over his Divine form. The whole room is filled with celestial beings!"

Baba got up and moved toward Goswami with outstretched arms. The assembled devotees stood fixed in their places and later described an unforgettable scene.

Goswami ran and fell devotedly at Baba's feet. Like a loving mother joyfully receiving her child after a long separation, Baba pulled Goswami to his heart. As he embraced Goswami, Baba transmitted a stream of spiritual power and inspiration to him. Goswami's body began to tremble, as if charged by a high voltage electric current. When Baba completed the transmission, Goswami began to collapse. The devotees caught hold of him and seated him near Baba. When Goswami later returned to normal consciousness, he asked Baba, "Why have you waited to call me to your Divine Presence? Why have I been deprived of your mercy until now?"

Baba replied, *"You are too heartless. Why did you come so late?"* Hearing this, Goswami understood how much Baba loved and had missed him and shed tears of joy.

By this time, a large number of people had gathered outside to meet Goswami. When one of Goswami's disciples asked Baba's permission to excuse Goswami to meet with these devotees, Baba readily said to Vijay, *"You are not only dear to me. Everyone seems to be eager to meet you, so go and meet them."*

After this historic meeting, Vijay Krishna Goswami paid a rich tribute to Baba with the following statement:

"In my lifelong experience of meeting many saints and sages in wide variety of ashrams, temples, and pilgrim centers, I have never met a yogi of his spiritual greatness. His spiritual stature is beyond human comprehension.

"Brahmachari Baba Lokenath's wish is final. He can leave his mortal body at any moment he wishes or retain it for eternity. The Grace that Baba has showered on me within a moment is enough for all my spiritual growth."

Goswami also said that Baba Lokenath had told him in confidence, *"It is good you have come. You take up the responsibility of completing my work. I shall go."* Then Baba suddenly looked at Goswami's body and changed his mind, saying, *"No it is not possible. Your body is not fit enough to carry my responsibility. I have to first prepare you for this task."*

Throughout his life, Goswami repeatedly told his many disciples and devotees, "Baradi is the birthplace of my spiritual life. In Baba Lokenath, I have seen the manifestation of Supreme Divinity. A saint of this stature rarely comes down from the Himalayas to the lower plane. Baba Lokenath has revealed himself in three different Divine forms of Mother Gayatri, in the three Sandhyas, Dawn, Midday and Dusk."

Vijay Krishna Goswami

KULADANANDA AND HIS DIARY

Goswami began preaching about Baba's Divinity throughout Bengal. When Goswami's own disciples heard their beloved Guru praising Baba so highly, they wanted to meet Baba to have his darshan. One such disciple was Kuladananda. After hearing about the greatness and glory of the Mahayogi Baba Lokenath, he was anxious to meet him. When he sought permission from his Master, Vijay Krishna said, "Go to him, but when you meet him do not talk or ask anything. He will tell you himself what is needed for you."

Kuladananda left for Baradi with his elder brothers and Tarakanta Ganguly. Tarakanta later came to be known as Brahmananda Bharati. The omniscient Baba knew about the visit of the devotees, so like a compassionate mother waiting for her children to come, he did not close the doors of his cottage that night. When they reached the ashram, Baba said to them. *"I did not close the doors of the cottage and have been waiting especially for you. Now you can take some food and then rest."*

The next morning the devotees went to Baba and prostrated themselves at his feet. Baba said to Kuladananda's elder brother, *"Earn money and selflessly spend it for suffering people."* Baba made it clear that earning and spending money should not be considered an obstacle to the spiritual aspirant. What matters is the attitude with which the money is used. Money becomes a curse to those who want to make it simply to satisfy their own material desires. This brings bondage. A true seeker wants to cultivate the spirit of selflessness and a compassionate heart and shares with the less privileged children of the Divine.

Kuladananda was sitting outside in the veranda. Baba called him. Baba asked Kuladananda to sit next to him and said, *"Are you not in the habit of writing in your personal diary everyday?"* Kuladananda kept a diary, but he did not understand how Baba knew this. Baba continued, *"In your diary you can note my following remarks. Renounce comforts and luxuries."* Baba then explained his meaning to Kuladananda.

"On the path of God Realization, the discipline that householders have to pass through is not the same as that of renunciate monks. For the renunciate, the path requires rising above the identification with the body by practicing an austere life. If a renounced monk in the initial phase of sadhana does not consciously endeavor to regulate eating habits, the company he keeps, the clothes he wears, and all such things, then the ego will pose subtle problems on the path. Attachment to the body will also be increased." Baba advised the renunciate to take only the bare necessities to keep the body fit for practice.

Kuladananda Brahmachari

Baba said further, *"If you ever feel depressed, come here and ask my advice. You can write to me. Do not worry and nourish negative ideas unnecessarily. You will be successful in your spiritual quest.*

"You are suffering from a colic pain in your stomach are you not? Come, I shall rub my hand on it and it shall be cured." In the next moment Baba said, *"This pain you have is due to your prarabdha karma* (the result of deeds in previous births). *If I rub my hand on it, it will be cured, but you would only have to suffer the condition again in the next life. Do not take any medicines. They will only further aggravate your condition. At the end of this prarabdha, the pain will go automatically. If it becomes intolerable you can rub fresh soil on it and the pain will subside."*

Kuladananda had been very depressed about his condition because it was a great obstacle to his meditation. Baba's comments about prarabdha karma remind the seeker that on the path of Truth one must bear with patience the pains of the body and agonies of the mind during the practice of meditation. Although Kuladananda lived the regulated life of a renunciate, spending hours of the day absorbed in worship of the Lord, he still had to undergo and accept intolerable colic pain due to the karma that he had accumulated from previous births. Baba taught that one must have patience and tolerance to withstand the prarabdha and the force with which it comes.

RENUNCIATION, ENJOYMENT AND SELF-RESTRAINT

Baba instructed Baradakanta, Kuladananda's second brother, differently. Baba told him, *"Earn money, enjoy life and finish up your prarabdha."* After hearing Baba's unique instruction, Baradakanta questioned him, "Don't you think that the injunction of the shastra of 'upabhog' (physical enjoyment) only intensifies rather than discourages one from sensual pleasure?"

Baba's reply is immensely valuable for householder seekers. Baba said, *"I have asked you to finish your karma through 'bhog' and not 'upabhog'. The difference between the two is like the husband and the lover. When you transgress the instruction of the scriptures and enjoy the life of the senses without proper control that becomes 'upabhog', illicit pleasure. This can never give you peace. However, you can attain peace through pleasure with a sense of control and respect for scriptural injunctions. This is 'bhog'. Your relationship with your wife insofar that it is in accordance with the shastra is never wrong and will never bar you from spiritual experience. If you do this, the prarabdha, the tendencies with which you were born, will be burned."*

This instruction of Baba's should be deeply contemplated by all seekers. According to Baba, it would be both impractical and harmful to advise ordinary individuals to give up the world of the senses before they have come to terms with their sensual tendencies. Many well-intentioned people join monasteries, becoming monks and nuns before they are ready. They suppress their tendencies in vain. This approach is not only ineffective; it is harmful. When one suppresses, it is only a matter of time before the tendencies resurface and the aspirant becomes either unbalanced or falls prey to desire. There are many monks who are not as advanced as householders because they are unable to keep their vows. Renunciation must come from the deepest level and not until the tendencies have been successfully restrained.

Suppression has an unconscious effect because of its refusal to acknowledge that the desires exist. The restrained mind longs for a higher purpose. Sacrifice is more spontaneous and conscious. The desire for God is experienced as an inner burning which consumes the desires of the lower nature. In the presence of inner bliss, the senses let go of their outer attachments and rest peacefully, absorbed in the Divine. Baba Lokenath, the practical prophet, warns against the unrestrained life of the senses while encouraging humanity to reach the exalted heights of spiritual life through the regulation of sensual pleasures.

The ordinary person indulges the senses without much restraint, following the unconscious dictates of an impure mind and intellect. It is no wonder that in the midst of material plenty there is so much spiritual poverty in the world. The deliberate refusal to heed the words of the Masters and the Holy Scriptures creates harmful vibrations in the entire cosmic system. We thus invite the wrath of Mother Nature, who will have no other alternative but to resort to mass destruction in order to re-establish true human values and proportion to life.

Self-restraint should not evoke negative reaction. It is absolutely positive. Through the exercise of restraint, we are shown a higher life.

Human beings were not born to live the unregulated life of instinct that animals do. We are to live consciously, in order to experience Ultimate Truth. The experience of true, unlimited joy can occur, provided the senses are not given complete freedom. Conscious restraint promotes the higher evolution of consciousness and the descent of Divine Grace.

Do not serve the instincts of your imperfect mind. Turn your mind and its energies toward the light of the Divine and the Masters to be transformed. If human society would follow the instructions of the saints and sages of the ages, if it revered and respected the principles of the Higher Truths they embodied, we would not suffer the anguish of societal disease. The Beloved reveals his mission on Earth through both renunciate monks and householders. Both work together to bring about the cosmic development of an integrated human society which honors all life as Divine.

Kuladananda was grateful for Baba's advice. In later years he published one of the most outstanding spiritual records of a practicing brahmacharin entitled, *"Sri Sri Satguru Sanga,"* in which he further describes his experience of Baba.

"Brahmachari Baba's eyes never blink. Anyone who attempted to look into Baba's eyes for more than a few minutes would faint. Yogis from the Himalayan and Tibetan regions would visit Baba's ashram in their "astral" bodies at night, leaving their gross bodies in the caves, to take lessons in advanced yoga. The doors of Baba's room remained closed in the evening. No one was permitted to enter Baba's room at night. Those who did out of curiosity had terrifying experiences."

Kuladananda's account once again illustrates the height of Baba Lokenath's Yogic state. Throughout the day, Baba would sit in the ashram with the doors open. He welcomed the multitudes with all of their problems and showered them with his blessings. At night, however, he played a different role. He was Master to the highly evolved yogis of the Himalayas and Tibet. Thus, he was known as the Yogi of Yogis, the Yogeshwara, the Incarnation and embodiment of the ultimate perfection of Yoga, the Yogavatar.

MEDITATION

Dedicate a day to making a new beginning in the practice of self-restraint. Begin the day rereading the segment of this chapter with the heading, "Renunciation, Enjoyment and Self-Restraint." In prayer, contemplate the highest purposes of your life. Make them real and vivid. Feel the blessings those purposes fulfilled would bring to you, to those you love, and to the world. Notice wherever their fulfillment is obstructed by desire. Look to see if, and how, you suppress desire. Do you condemn yourself in relation to desire? Anticipate any problematic desires that may arise in the coming day. Establish clearly in your mind and heart the higher good you want in your life. Ask Baba to help you to hold the vibrant, higher good uppermost in your mind and heart whenever a desire presents itself. Then, throughout the day, in the moment of desire, call on Baba for help. Offer the desire—as a sacrifice, freely given—into the joyful fire of your longing for the higher, greater, truer good you aspire to.

Cultivate awareness of the deeper spiritual yearnings which problematic desires are a substitute for. Pray sincerely to Baba whenever you are in the grip of a desire for the fulfillment of the deeper reality, rather than a superficial, substitute indulgence.

CHAPTER 11

THE MYSTERIOUS WAYS OF THE SATGURU

DURING HIS LAST few years in the physical body, we see Baba in the role of the Universal Teacher. Between 1886 and 1890, Baba not only distributed material benefits to the many devotees who flooded the ashram premises each day, but he also initiated those fortunate few who came to him in search of Eternal Truth.

Baba's blessings, however, were not limited to those who had direct contact with him. His Divine Grace was always available to those who sincerely sought truth. Often he would travel in his astral body in search of spiritual aspirants who were engaged in the practice of yoga. A steady stream of grace would flow to them from his subtle Divine form as he instructed them in the higher principles of yoga. Those seekers who received this subtle instruction would frequently find their way to Baba's ashram. Though Baba's devotees often questioned him about his work on the subtle plane, he said little about it.

RAJANI BRAHMACHARI

Rajani Brahmachari, who became the most dedicated and ardent devotee of Baba, heard about him from Vijay Krishna Goswami. Rajani

Brahmachari described his first meeting with Baba Lokenath in 1887 as follows.

"After having a fresh morning bath, Vrindavan Chandra Dey and I left for Baba's ashram. We were told that Baba always kept sugar candy in his mouth, so we had sweets to take to him. When we arrived, we found the ashram of Brahmachari Baba to be very much like the hermitage of the Rishis in ancient Vedic days. It was a tranquil place, surrounded on all sides with flowering plants and trees which offered shade to visitors. A bael tree adjacent to Baba's cottage was the center of attraction. I had never seen a bael tree of that kind in my life. The tree was tall with branches that stretched in every direction and resembled a large banyan tree. A raised round platform was erected around the root of the tree.

"When I entered Baba's room, I found myself in his presence. Baba was sitting quietly as a woman worshipped his feet with flowers. Before long, the woman finished her worship. I placed the packet of sweets before him and prostrated. As I touched his Divine feet with my forehead, I was filled with the sweet fragrance from his body. It was a heavenly scent that cannot be compared to any earthly material thing.

"I fell into a deep trance and remained prostrated at his feet for over fifteen minutes, totally forgetting the external world. After I regained normal consciousness, I sat on the right hand side of Baba and looked at his eyes, which had a godly look. As time passed, I noticed that he never blinked.

Rajanikanta Brahmachari

"Baba pointed to a few floor mats kept at the corner of the veranda and said in a somewhat harsh tone, *'Why do you sit here? Go and sit there!'* I answered him softly in surrender, saying, 'I have the desire of sitting at your feet.' Baba replied in the same harsh tone, *'Desires are the cause of all miseries.'* As I contemplated the meaning of his words, I saw that Baba's non-blinking eyes became fixed. There was practically no sign of respiration. He sat as still as a picture in his gomukhasana posture, without any sign of life. I could feel that his body was there, but that he had left the body and gone beyond to realms unknown to humans. I was face to face with a Living God who was in the world. His presence awed me. I had heard about samadhi, the transcendental consciousness, but had never seen anyone in that Divine state.

"Fifteen minutes passed. I was totally absorbed, forgetful about the passage of time, flooded with ecstasy. I kept gazing at his radiant physical form. Just as he became still, suddenly he again showed signs of returning to this world."

ON THE QUESTION OF CELIBACY IN A SPIRITUAL MARRIAGE

After Baba inquired about the details of Rajani's family background and learned of the death of Rajani's wife, Baba said, *"I recommend that you marry again."* Rajani Chakraborty, who was determined not to marry again, replied, "I shall not be able to carry out your orders." Baba asked, *"Why not?"* Rajani answered, "I see all women as mother." He told Baba how, one day, his wife came to him and entreated him to promise that they would not have any more physical contact as husband and wife, but rather continue as brother and sister. Rajani was elated with the change, which he knew would be a great help to his spiritual growth. He declared to his wife that from that day forward she would be his mother. She readily agreed.

Hearing this, Baba Lokenath, was moved and said lovingly, *"Is the Golden Age back again? Then why have you come to me? I should have gone to you."*

Baba's response highlights an important spiritual teaching. Baba was deeply pleased to hear that both Rajani and his wife had chosen a life of celibacy even though they were married. Baba always stressed the necessity for sensual restraint in the life of a true spiritual aspirant. Truth can only be achieved through the determined will power to surrender at the feet of the Divine and this comes, in part, as a natural result of celibacy.

Rajani's case serves as perfect example of spiritual marriage. That path, however, may be difficult for western seekers because of the cultural emphasis that is placed on sexual gratification. Seekers should realize that a spiritual marriage does not occur without effort. The spiritual journey for the householder begins with a mutual commitment to a higher aim. Generally speaking, in the initial stages of marriage, the attraction that the husband and wife have for each other is expressed through the senses. It has a greater power over the individuals than the Divine qualities of love and devotion. Eventually this will change. If it does not and the married couple cannot transcend their passions, it is important that they remember that any internal conflict or self-condemnation they might feel is ultimately more harmful than the indulgence itself.

Spiritual seekers may find themselves torn between the suppression of sexual desire and indulgence. Neither of these alternatives can bring happiness. In the final analysis, the sincere spiritual seeker must willingly face the impossibility of ever solving the dilemma of his craving and surrender it to the Divine. Baba teaches that the passions can be spiritualized through the repetition of God's name. If the aspirants truly love God and are sincere, then the transformation will gradually occur. It is only through the grace of God that the seeming dualities of flesh and spirit can be reconciled because they are in truth, one.

When the desire to experience God as a living reality grows in the seeker's heart, the seeker spontaneously draws away from sensual pleasure, which seems increasingly limited. The seeker moves more and more toward the light of awakening Divinity. Filled with bliss, sexual energy is transformed into Divine energy. When this occurs, marriage to the Divine takes place within the soul, and the marriage relationship fulfills its destiny. Husband and wife are drawn together because of the Divine Love that is felt in their hearts and seen in each other. Having merged in the purest sense, they share a greater vision of life and become exemplars of Living Truth.

The issue of sex troubles many spiritual seekers. Questions often asked include, "What is wrong with sensual indulgence? Isn't sexual expression, for example, part of nature? Isn't it a deep expression of love for many?"

To address these questions, a wider view must be taken. It has been said again and again that the problem is man's fundamental ignorance of the Truth. Human beings have never really learned or accepted that our primary destiny is to realize God. God-Realization is the ultimate purpose of our existence. That has been the message of the saints and sages from time immemorial. Without understanding our higher nature and purpose, however, we are left only with our senses, which operate in an endless, cyclical pattern.

Desire, in excitation, demands satisfaction. Satisfaction, in turn, fans the flame of increased desire. This leaves us chasing the objects of our desire, spending most, if not all, of our energy and attention in the process. The world we can see, touch and feel becomes an absorbing, singular reality, leaving little left over for pursuit of the Divine. Because the Divine is subtle, it easily drops from consciousness entirely. The consequent absorption in the limited, material world is the root of the problem.

Religion has admonished humankind throughout the ages to restrain its sensual impulses. In many instances, however, this prescription has been delivered without explanation. Without understanding the wisdom of the law, the law becomes a cruel imposition. After all, if we operate from the assumption that nothing exists beyond the senses, then it is natural that we would rebel against that which forbids us to enjoy the source of our pleasure in life. If we could capture a glimpse of the spiritual treasures which await us, nothing could restrain us from doing everything in our power to claim our Divine inheritance. In that glimpse, we would realize that nothing in the transitory world could compare in any way to the experience of the love, freedom, and bliss that awaits us.

These same questions about sexual expression and its role may be looked at from another perspective. If we were to travel around the world, or even to outer space, then we would necessarily travel by air, ship or spacecraft. Without fuel, these vehicles, no matter how sophisticated, would not be able to move.

So it is in the spiritual process. We require fuel to reach our spiritual destination. In this case, the fuel is the allotment of energy that each is given at birth. Without this energy, one can do nothing. In its primal form, it is experienced as sexual energy. Through the practice of spiritual discipline, that energy rises through the chakras (the spiritual centers located along the spinal cord) until it reaches the crown, signaling the Realization of God. The directed use of this energy brings great spiritual reward. Each of us has the power of free will and can use the energy in whatever way we choose. If the energy is misdirected through anger, sensual over-indulgence, greed, anxiety, and similar expressions, it dissipates and is not available for transformation into higher states of consciousness. We will be unable to experience the bliss and freedom that is our birthright. Instead, we will have to return lifetime after lifetime until we learn through experience the value and purpose of this energy. Thus begins our journey home.

Rajani Chakraborty had learned to restrain his senses. He received initiation from Baba and became known as Rajani Brahmachari. In Rajani's life, Baba masterfully demonstrated his skill as Supreme Guru. He knew exactly what was needed for the progress of his disciples and how to approach them according to their individual character. He did whatever was necessary to lead his beloved children to their Divine goal. As the following stories reveal, however, Baba was often mischievous and playful in the ways he taught and coaxed his devotees to higher consciousness.

BABA'S CURE FOR HABIT AND ADDICTION

Rajani had the habit of smoking tobacco. One day, he had the urge to smoke tobacco three times while with Baba. Each time, Baba said to him, *"What kind of a devotee are you? You don't even offer me tobacco?"* Each time, Rajani prepared tobacco in his own cup and offered it to Baba. Baba then offered the tobacco back to him. Rajani quietly accepted it. Then, as he prepared to leave the room to smoke outside, Baba called to him, *"You have to smoke right in front of me."* After this happened three times, Rajani's lifelong habit of smoking left him forever. Baba, in his inimitable, compassionate and playful way, had helped Rajani rid himself of an unhealthy habit that was interfering with his spiritual growth.

Baba's guidance of Rajani, though playful and tender, has beautiful layers of meaning, instruction, and hope for anyone struggling with an addiction. The Satguru does not demand that we bring only our best, complete sacrifices to the altar of his presence. He asks for ALL that we are, good and bad, strong and incorrigibly weak. Baba tells us, through Rajani, that we must never allow our faults, or our guilt and shame for having them, to keep us away from the altar of the Divine, even for an instant. Instead, we are to bring our most stubborn self-indulgences to him, in the very instant of our failure to control them — again and again, if we have to — until we are healed by his grace. There is no sin so great, no weakness so entrenched, that the Satguru cannot and will not heal in those who remain lovingly in his Presence.

Whenever Baba wanted a devotee to come to him at Baradi, he would not send word through anyone else. He inwardly called the devotee. The devotee receiving the subtle call would feel a deep urge to run to Baba. Once, Rajani received such a call to meet Baba at Baradi and he was told to leave without his umbrella. Rajani immediately set out on foot for Baradi in the hot sun, obediently leaving his umbrella behind. The distance from Dacca to Baradi was great and the road was uneven and full of stone chips that were difficult to walk on.

The sudden call may have been Baba's method of testing his disciple. Could Rajani accept Baba's order without complaint and act upon it? Rajani did so willingly. Though he was barefoot, he was surprised to find that he was not bothered by the road or the sweltering heat. He felt no fatigue at all. Instead, he felt refreshed -- and when he touched Baba's feet, his entire being was filled with peaceful bliss.

Baba would sometimes get very wild if anyone failed to perform his duty. On one such occasion he told Rajani, *"I am not Rishi Janak. Rishi Janak never cared when one side was burnt. I abuse one person, beat the other, and take yet another on my lap."*

King Janaka is an example of Rajarishi, the seer-king in Indian mythology. Through the path of detached action (Karma Yoga), Janaka had reached such a desireless state of spiritual consciousness that, although he was a king immersed in material pleasures, he was untouched and remained free of attachment. *"Janaka never cared when one side was burnt"* refers to a time that Janaka's palace was on fire. Everyone was running for his or her lives. Janaka, unperturbed by the danger, remained unconcerned and laughed loudly over the whole incident. This is a high spiritual state, but Baba had reached a state that was still more advanced, the state of Brahmarishi. Of yogis in the category of Knower of Brahman, he was Brahmavidvaristha, a Supreme Knower of the Supreme Brahman.

"I abuse one person, beat the other, and take yet another on my lap" refers to Baba's state of absolute detachment. To teach, he acted like the most attached householder, though he was completely detached. He responded spontaneously to external situations, as all Enlightened Ones do. He chastized when there was a need for it, while soothing the pain of his other suffering children with motherly affection.

The Enlightened Ones are not merely an embodiment of detachment. Deep compassion flowers in them, leading them to assume the role of world teacher. They accept the pain of everyday people while patiently teaching the path that leads to transcendence. They show the path by which every human being can leave the miseries of mundane life behind. Jesus, Buddha, Mahavira, Sri Chaitanya, Sri Ramakrishna are all examples of this level of Divine manifestation. They are worshipped all over the world as Incarnations of God because that is exactly what they are.

Those who take refuge in Baba should be aware that, although Baba is pleased to grant the material wishes of his children, he would also not hesitate to chastize them for their errors.

Baba's inimitable and careful guidance of Rajani continued.

Baba once said to Rajani, *"The causes of all attachment are known to me. Why allow them to overpower you?"* Rajani asked, "May I know the causes?" Baba replied, *"The shot of abusive and insulting words, the shot of the pain of separation from loved ones, and the shot of pain from losing wealth, if one can bear with patience these three shots, he can transcend even death."* Here, Baba was referring to the painful and piercing shot of an arrow.

At one point, Baba gave Rajani an unusual lesson on detachment from the insult and judgment of others. Rajani's lesson is our lesson, too, on the unpredictable ways in which a Guru may test and use the disciple as an example in teaching others.

One day, Baba instructed Rajani to wear a loincloth as an undergarment and to use costly shawls to cover his body. This was to signify that Rajani had reached a state of detachment toward materialistic things in the world.

Baba, as the Master, had devised a test of Rajani's devotion to his Guru which would teach both Rajani and other devotees an important lesson. Baba spread a rumor to the followers of Rajani who often visited the ashram that Rajani was a hypocrite. *"Rajani says that I have instructed him to wear a Kaupinam (loincloth), but that is a lie. He is trying to glorify himself by wearing one."*

Baba's statement caused great confusion in the minds of Rajani's followers, who soon began to doubt the genuineness of his spiritual attainment. Even those who had been most attached to Rajani began withdrawing themselves from his company. They believed Baba's accusation because they knew that it was only through his grace that Rajani was progressing so quickly on the path of yoga. Hearing Baba speak so disparagingly about his own disciple, they fell prey to Baba's play. They, too, began speaking ill of Rajani, as Baba expected they would.

The rumor continued for some time. Rajani, knew that he was being tested by his Gurudev and remained indifferent to the whole issue. When the time was ripe, Rajani went to Baba and asked, "It appears that you are telling your devotees that you never asked me to wear a loincloth and that I have worn the loincloth with the intention of glorifying myself as a saint to the people." Baba replied, *"Yes, I have said it."* Rajani asked, "Why have you told this lie?" Baba replied, *"Since I gave you the loincloth you have been spreading the greatness of your Guru, and I am being disturbed too often as a result. They do not allow me to rest in peace."*

The test of trust in the Guru, which Baba administered to Rajani, was extremely difficult. Only one who had a sense of detachment and great trust in the Guru could pass such a trial successfully. Rajani never lost his trust and devotion to his. He merely said to others challenging him, *"Brahmachari Baba is all merciful. Whatever he says must be for my good."* This unquestioning surrender to the will of the Guru must be the attitude of the disciple.

Baba later asked Rajani, *"Have you understood the secret of the loincloth?" It serves as the rod of punishment. It helps to keep the mind in proper control and does not allow the mind to indulge in its lower nature."*

The reason behind Baba's lie was gradually revealed to everyone. Rajani developed great compassion through his deep trust in Baba and his earnest efforts to be a true disciple. He began healing many of incurable diseases. Those who could not go to Baradi told Rajani about their problems. Rajani always blessed them in the name of Lokenath and the miracles would occur through Baba's grace.

Baba Lokenath was training Rajani to be sensitive and vigilant regarding activities which might bring him fame and hinder his spiritual progress. He also humbled more selfish, less developed devotees by revealing their weaknesses of character and discipleship, all by exemplifying genuine discipleship through Rajani's tolerance and reverence.

Baba Lokenath saw Rajani's advancement. The time had come for him to leave his home and have a separate cottage in isolation, so that he could go into deeper realms of the spirit. One day, Baba asked Rajani, *"Can't you have a room like mine to sit in meditation?"* He further explained, *"Until you sever all connections with your relations at home and retreat into a deep, meditative state with a single-pointed mind, you cannot realize yourself. You must hasten to do this to reach the final state."*

A short time later, Rajani Brahmachari left home for good and went to live in Wari Yogashrama. He eventually established his own ashram near Dacca. He lived there for the rest of his life absorbed in his sadhana. After Baba left his mortal body, Rajani served as the chosen instrument of Baba Lokenath.

As a spiritual Master of Masters, Baba also orchestrated a similar lila with the disciples and devotees of Vijay Krishna Goswami. For a period, when any of Goswami's disciples or devotees came for Baba's darshan, Baba would speak badly about Goswami. This was very difficult for the disciples and other devotees to understand.

One day, Baba was seated, surrounded by a large number of devotees and disciples. Suddenly, his attention was fixed at the gate of the ashram where a devotee named Sridhar was approaching the cottage. The moment Baba saw the devotee coming, his mood changed. He drew the attention of the assembled devotees to the stranger and said, *"Here comes one of the disciples of Jivan Krishna. He is wasting his life by following the wrong master. If this is not the truth, then how is it that I find no development in his spiritual state, in spite of the fact that he is sincerely following his Guru?"*

In *"Sri, Sri Satguru Sanga,"* Kuladananda speaks about this disciple, who was madly in love with his master, Vijay Krishna Goswami. The love and steadfast devotion that Sridhar had for his Gurudev is an example for all disciples to imitate. Through Sridhar, Baba demonstrates the qualities of a true disciple: love, reverence, devotion, and deep trust in the master. Through this lila, we see that all of the actions and words of the Enlightened Ones are charged with deep spiritual significance and instruction.

Sridhar came for Baba's darshan after hearing a great deal from his master about Baba's high spiritual state. He was shocked to the core to hear the sage insulting his beloved master. Vijay Krishna was the embodiment of Godhood for him. He could not tolerate a single word of insult to his dear master. It was his conviction and deep understanding that to speak ill about the Guru, or to listen to anyone insult him was suicidal for any disciple. He would not allow anyone to commit this blunder. He could not imagine that the person about whom his Gurudev spoke so highly could degrade himself to such a low level by criticizing his master before so many people!

To add more fuel to the fire of the rage burning in the heart of Sridhar, Baba added, *"If you believe that your Guru has any power of truth in him then why do you keep silent? Your Guru is blind, and you too are blind. Yours is the story of the blind leading the blind. I rather suggest that you leave your Guru and come to me. See for yourself how I will grant you Divine visions in no time."*

Sridhar was blind with rage. He picked up a large stick and ran toward Baba with every intention of beating him to death. To him, death was the just and correct punishment for such a contemptible act on the part of a monk.

The devotees, concerned with the sudden unpleasant turn in the situation, ran to Sridhar, trying to dissuade him from such a mad act. In the meantime, Baba left his seat and went to Sridhar with outstretched arms, embracing him with immense love. Baba's was demonstrating to the disciples present, as well as to disciples everywhere, the depth of love that a disciple should have for his master.

Baba took Sridhar to his room, where he showered him with affection, saying, *"I have given you so much pain and spoken ill about your Guru only to see this much from you. I am deeply pleased with the depth of love you have for your master. You are blessed. You have rightly developed Guru-bhakti, wholehearted devotion for the master. Those who follow the path of spiritual discipline without having this kind of deep love for the master will never have Ultimate Truth revealed to them. Because you have that, you will reach your goal."*

Baba blessed Sridhar with all his heart and said, *"The reason I criticize Jivan Krishna (Vijay Krishna Goswami) whenever his disciples and devotees come to me is known to me and your master. That is the reason these days that he does not allow his close disciples and devotees to come to me. No one will understand the pain that Jivan Krishna suffers for his disciples and devotees. How can the common man realize who Jivan Krishna is, why he has come, and why he is so selflessly distributing rich spiritual treasures to the common man? When you reach that stage of perfection through your unconditional surrender to the Guru, you will realize that Jivan Krishna and I are one and the same in the realm of Eternal Divine Play."*

Baba finished speaking and in the next moment transcended to the world beyond. His body remained on the seat like a lifeless statue, without the slightest pulsation of life. He was in a state of samadhi. Sitting next to him, Sridhar felt inexpressible bliss. A brilliant radiance surrounded the body of Baba and the entire room was filled with a sublime fragrance. Immersed in Divine intoxication, Sridhar closed his eyes. When he opened them, he saw his beloved Master Vijay Krishna Goswami sitting in the place of Baba. Drunk with ecstasy, he prostrated himself at his master's feet. When he raised his head again, Baba Lokenath was sitting there with a Divine smile.

Baba had rewarded Sridhar's love and devotion to Goswami with an experience that elevated him to a new level of understanding. Baba had shown Sridhar the literal truth of his statement that Baba and Vijay Krishna were truly One and the same in the realm of Eternal Divine Play.

This dramatic Divine Play of Baba dispels the darkness in the minds of the followers of Satgurus who fear that if they bow and respect other Satgurus, it could mean a shift of loyalty. The Guru Gita proclaims, *"mad guru shree jagadguru"* — my Guru is the Universal Master. You must have single pointed devotion to your Master. Keep the heart open, also, to receive the light from all the Illumined Ones. For beyond the plane of the material body, they are One in the ultimate ground of pure consciousness.

MEDITATION

Most devotees take our lives and God so seriously that we are weighted down and utterly miss the delight with which God and Guru would prefer to play with us. Ask Baba to help you release ALL heaviness. Then, as you go through the day, look for ways to play with others, yourself and your circumstances. Imagine it is all Baba coming to play with you. Where is the joy hiding? How is the teaching disguised? If you find yourself in circumstances which normally produce stress or upset, step back. See it all as Baba coming to play with you, whimsically coaxing you to lighten up, to enjoy absurdity, to find greater joy, and cultivate lightness of being.

CHAPTER 12

THE CLOSEST DISCIPLES

SATGURU LOKENATH DREW his devotees from a variety of sources. Many initially came only for relief from their mundane problems. Touched by his grace, however, many who were rid of physical obstacles were also drawn into realms of mystic light. Turning to the lives of Baba's close disciples who came to Baradi and who reached a high state of yoga, it is important to note that most were householders. Baba drew them to Baradi and guided them to a life of true renunciation. He did not create a band of sannyasins, robed in saffron, living the life of the renunciate. Baba worked with ordinary householders and lifted them to the life of brahmacharin and the state of sannyas as a direct message for the coming millennium. There is no need to run away from home, wife, and children, or material possessions. The need is to renounce attachment through the possessive love of the Satguru. Baba showed that with the grace of the Satguru and the disciple's intense devotion and perseverance, God-Realization is not a distant dream. It is a practical reality. By being truly surrendered to the Satguru, one can reach the Divine home.

GWALINI MA

An old woman named Kamala lived in a small cottage near the ashram of Baba Lokenath. She earned her meager living by selling milk from her only asset, a sickly cow.

One day, she came for Baba's darshan and brought him a small offering of cow's milk. When Baba saw her approaching, he was delighted. He invited her inside the room, saying, *"How is it that the mother could remain away from the child for such a long time?"* The old woman had a deep motherly feeling the moment she saw Baba and took him in her lap as if Baba was her own son. Baba called her Gwalini Ma.

Through the grace of Baba, Gwalini Ma shouldered many responsibilities in the ashram despite her advanced age. She cared for visitors by distributing prasad to them. She also administered to the needs of the ailing patients who came in large numbers to seek Baba's blessings. Baba developed so much confidence in Gwalini Ma that he never did anything concerning the management of the ashram without consulting her.

Baba prepared and ate his morning food (balbhog) himself on the northern side of the veranda, in front of his one room cottage. The afternoon bhog or meal was prepared by Gwalini Ma, who always covered her mouth with cloth during preparation. She would allow no one inside until Baba had eaten. Today, wherever Baba Lokenath is worshipped and bhog, a food offering, is made, it is expected that devotees cover their mouths as was the custom strictly followed at the Baradi Ashram.

Gwalini Ma

Gwalini Ma was blessed to observe at close proximity the rare phenomena of the Enlightened One. She shared Baba's lilas whenever devotees requested her to do so. Once, when lightning shook the foundation of the ashram, one devotee became quite alarmed. Gwalini Ma calmly told the devotee that the power of the storm was only slight compared to the power of Baba. She assured the frightened devotee that there was no need for concern. She explained that after spending a long time in the ashram in the presence of Baba, she had found that no power in heaven or on earth could do any harm to Baba's devotees.

The devotee wanted to know where Baba was on that stormy night. Gwalini Ma replied that no one could say where he was or was not. Even though she was very close to him, she confessed that she could not understand anything about his unpredictable movements and manifestations.

Sometimes Baba would be seen sitting on his usual seat, then in the next moment he would no longer be there. Sometimes when he was found in the room, his body was there but he was not. At other times, Baba was found to be manifesting in different places in his tangible form at the same time.

Gwalini Ma told the devotee, "Not a single thought in the mind goes unnoticed by him. During my first days with him, I was frightened lest he should come to know all that played in my mind. Sometimes he would say, and usually pretend, that he knew nothing. Later when I came to know that he is sitting in my heart, watching all my thoughts, I began to accept the situation with ease.

"I have realized that whatever I do, it is his doing. Whatever I think, it is his thinking. I have no responsibility whatsoever. I am just at ease leaving the whole responsibility with him."

BRAHMANANDA BHARATI

In addition to Gwalini Ma, another close associate and disciple of Baba's was Brahmananda Bharati. In the hearts of most of Baba's devotees, there is a question about the rebirth of Guru Bhagwan and his return to Baba. Many believe that he came as Brahmananda Bharati, while others believe that he was Rajani Brahmachari. Both disciples advanced considerably on the spiritual path through the Grace of Baba.

Brahmananda Bharati was a householder first known as Tarakanta Ganguli. He was a man of scriptural knowledge and a seeker on the path of Jnana. Through the grace of Baba, he, too, was transformed and in later years became the ardent disciple who wrote "*Siddha Jivani*" in Bengali, a book on the life and Divine Play of Baba.

When he first met Baba at Baradi, Baba asked him the reason for his coming. He answered like a knowledgeable philosopher that, "I am dying in the pit dug by me. I am stuck in the mundane plane by my own will and caught in the trap laid by my own ignorance. I am bound by the fetters of attachment and cannot overcome this bondage. You are an Enlightened One. Why not grace me in such a way that I become free from this bondage of maya? If you do it, then kindly reveal the technique by which you have transcended this bondage so that I, too, can transcend this illusion created by nature."

Brahmananda Bharati Mathuramohan Chakraborty

Baba answered his question very simply. "Transcend Maya by worshipping Her."

With his mind full of information gathered through the various scriptures, Tarakanta Ganguli thought that he could conquer Nature with the grace of Baba. But Baba had pulled an invaluable gem from his bag of rich spiritual treasures and presented it to Tarakanta Ganguli.

Maya, Invincible Mother Nature, is the primal energy of existence. She can never be conquered. By worshipping her, by pleasing her through sadhana (spiritual discipline), one receives her Divine Grace. Lower nature is transformed and spontaneously transcends all bondage, ignorance, and attachment. Through worship, Maya ceases to be maya. She becomes Mahamaya, the Divine Herself, the

Universal Mother. The realization comes that She Alone is manifested in the entire creation, so who will conquer whom?

Tarakanta Ganguli argued, "But nature is inert. I don't want to worship inert nature."

Baba was quiet for some time, and then replied, *"The moth covers its own body with the silken fibers from its own mouth and remains bound within that cell. Nobody can help it come out of that. But when the moth in due course transforms itself into a butterfly, then it cuts open its own cell and comes out without anyone's help."*

With this example, Baba reminds us that we are bound by our own actions and thoughts. The mind, given to lower nature or to mundane materialistic attachments, remains bound. The same mind, boosted by spiritual discipline, transforms. Becoming pure mind, it is the gateway to liberation and brings the ultimate fulfillment of life.

Tarakanta grew in his profound faith and devotion to Baba. Baba initiated him and gave him the name of Brahmananada Bharati. After Baba's mahasamadhi, Tarakanta left his highly successful law practice and his ancestral home to settle in Varanasi in pursuit of his relentless longing for Self-Realization.

CHANDRA KISHORE CHAKRABORTY

Another noted follower of Baba's was Shri Chandra Kishore Chakraborty, a resident of Bikrompur. Once, Chandra Kishore came to Baradi, where he squatted outside Baba's room for nine consecutive days without food or water.

On the ninth night, Baba came out of his room. He called the ashram devotees, told them that he was feeling restless, and asked them to immediately offer some milk and candy to Chandra Kishore.

Chandra Kishore became Baba's devotee. He received the grace of performing miracles with the spiritual powers he had gained by squatting near Baba's room. He instantly cured many lame and ailing persons by throwing dust at them in the name of Baba Lokenath. Enjoying an increasingly wide popularity in Dacca, large numbers of people assembled at his residence. His ego, unfortunately, took hold. Ultimately, he lost his spiritual powers due to subsequent misdeeds.

Baba once said, *"I have everything with me. You only have to take it."* Chandra Kishore believed in the spiritual powers of Baba. But he enjoyed those powers and the fame they brought. Baba tested him during those nine days and granted him some spiritual power. Chandra Kishore, however, was not attuned to the true grace. He failed to practice the spiritual disciplines that would lead to purification of the body-mind and to the retention of the powers which Baba had transmitted to him. In time, the powers waned because his actions were motivated by selfish desire.

Chandra Kishore exemplifies why scriptures place so little importance on spiritual powers. The great saints have always warned against them. If misused, they cause the fall of the seeker. As Baba has said, *"Only in a state of egolessness can these powers become a true blessing to society at large."*

ABHAYA CHARAN CHAKRABORTY

Another seeker who had been spiritually uplifted by Baba's blessings was Abhaya Charan Chakraborty. Renouncing his family and all material possessions, Abhaya Charan Chakraborty became a wandering mendicant, a brahmacharin, who traveled extensively for seventeen years before making a pilgrimage to Baradi.

Baba did not easily grant his blessings to those who demanded spiritual bliss from him. Baba tested Abhaya. After a night's stay in the ashram, Abhaya presented himself to Baba, asking for his Divine Grace. Baba replied, *"Why have you come to me? You are a human being and I, too, am. You eat and attend to the call of nature, and I, too, eat and attend to the call of nature like anyone of you."*

Hearing this, Abhaya became convinced that Baba would not yield easily. He prostrated himself before Baba, hit his head three times, then angrily left Baba's presence. Baba immediately called him back and said, *"You will get food to eat."*

Abhaya was irritated and replied harshly, "I have not come here for food. I can go without food for several days, and for a Brahmin, a handful of rice can always be received in alms."

At that early hour of the morning, there was no food in the ashram. Baba could not stand that his child would have no food after fasting, so the food appeared. As Abhaya was leaving again, he met a young widow with her old mother coming to Baba with varieties of cooked food and sweets. Baba called Abhaya back affectionately, and offered him the food the women had brought.

The next day when Abhaya sat before Baba, Baba said, *"You have traveled in the hills and mountains for seventeen years. Have you received that for which you have been traveling?"*

The brahmacharin replied, "No I have not."

Then Baba took Abhaya's right wrist in his own hand and said, *"I have tied that in your hand for which you have been traveling. You need not move about anymore. What will you gain by mere traveling? Action is Brahman."* Then Baba pointed to Rajani Brahmachri, who was sitting beside him, and said, *"Go with him. See his work. He and I are one and the same."*

Baba's encounter with Abhaya instructs us about the path of karma yoga. Desireless action is yoga. Baba made it clear to all seekers that what is important is not visits to temples and holy pilgrimages. Rather, it is the mind and our attitude. Unless the mind gravitates toward the center within, to the Divine sitting deep in the heart of the seeker, the seeker will be unable to feel the Presence of the Divine, or to receive light from the higher domains of spiritual consciousness.

Baba taught that all action is inseparable from God, because it is the Divine who is the Doer in all things. In the words of Baba, *"Action is Brahman."* As the Cosmic Dancer, Lord Shiva cannot be separated from His dance. So also, all action performed in the awareness of God as the Doer is transformed into Divine Dance. The human doer disappears, absorbed in the Divine Doer. Action becomes worship, consciously transcending the imperfections of ego through selfless action and the ordinary human being becomes instrumental in working for the peace and blessedness of the world.

The Divine Will manifests as energy in everything around us. Becoming conscious of the Divine hiding in all circumstances, we align ourselves with the higher purposes of all that life gives us. All grumbling and negativity fall away. The clouds that shroud our mind gradually lift. Divine energy manifests through our mind with greater clarity, moving us toward perfection. If we behave rudely toward anyone, we unknowingly throw a mantle over their mind and our own. Instead of helping to lift the world, we perpetuate the darkness that enslaves the world. The Divine searches for the instrument which is always open to receive and give higher energy. Offering ourselves and all our actions to the Divine Doer, then surrendering the result of those actions to God, is the path of karma which never binds. Instead, it releases the soul from the bondage of Maya (illusion).

HARICHARAN CHAKRABORTY

The people of Baradi often called Baba Lokenath *"Kalpataru."* Since the *Kalpataru* is the wish-fulfilling tree of Hindu mythology, it was only natural. Baba fulfilled the longings of all who came to Him. In the life of a devotee named Haricharan Chakraborty, however, Baba manifested the *Kalpataru* Lila quite literally.

Haricharan was a successful attorney in the Judges Court at Dacca (Bangladesh). He was by nature gentle and devoted to God. At that time, Baba's fame was spreading all over Dacca due to Vijay Krishna Goswami. The story of Baba's unique yogic powers became familiar to all households.

Haricharan had been sincerely searching for an enlightened master who could guide him to Ultimate Truth. Hearing of Baba,

Haricharan was instantly drawn to him. Haricharan knew that mere practices of yoga techniques and chanting were not enough. He recognized immediately in the stories of Baba the enlightened Master who had come to take him home. He came running to Baradi.

Looking into Baba's intense, non-blinking eyes, Haricharan's mind was instantly stilled. He was speechless. The still, intuitive voice within him said, "Yes! He is the one that I have been looking for. The Rishi of the Vedic days is reborn. He was so close, yet I did not know!"

Haricharan prostrated himself at the feet of Baba and utterly surrendered for the rest of his life. Deeply moved by the depth of Haricharan's surrender and devotion, Baba accepted Haricharan as his close disciple. He took responsibility for dispelling all darkness and ignorance, and guided Haricharan on the path to Bliss.

Haricharan's intense love and intent practice made for quick progress. Pleased with Haricharan's *Guru-bhakti* (love of Guru), Baba presented Haricharan with Baba's own wooden sandals. Haricharan, in Sanskrit, means the Feet of Lord Hari. With this gift, Baba literally validated the name. For the rest of his life, Haricharan worshipped Baba's wooden sandals. After his death, Haricharan's wife took Baba's sandals to Varanasi. There, she, too, worshipped Baba's *paduka* (sandals) until her death.

Baba had previously presented his *paduka* to Vijay Krishna Goswami, who was already a saint of attainment. By giving his *paduka* to a householder, Baba demonstrated that any mind filled with love and surrender to the Satguru, can attain to His Lotus Feet. The *paduka* is a vibrant symbol of that reality.

Once, Haricharan's son Satyacharan was suffering from an incurable disease and was near death. Haricharan carried his dying son to the ashram of Baradi. Weeping, he left his son at Baba's feet. Baba asked Satyacharan to get up and move. He got up, completely free of the disease by the pure power of Baba's Divine Word.

Baba manifested his power to heal whenever the opportunity presented itself. At another time, Haricharan's youngest son Saradacharan was afflicted with a chronic disease. All treatments had failed. Haricharan was once again at the feet of his Master asking for mercy and the life of his child. Baba loved all members of Haricharan's family. Sarada was very dear to him. Baba gave Sarada the option to choose his own medicine. Sarada picked up a small branch of a creeper plant, which to the amazement of all the devotees present, cured him.

To one brother, Baba's word was the cure. To the other, Baba gave the power to choose his own medicine. In both cases, it was Baba's compassion and Divine energy that worked the miracles. As Baba said, time and time again, *"Whenever the devotees cry in agony and distress, my heart melts — and with that, my power flows to them and frees them from their miseries."*

One day, Baba said, *"Haricharan, I have become Kalpataru now. Take whatever you want from me."* Overwhelmed with joy that his beloved had opened the treasure house to him, both Hari and his wife knew that there was nothing more they needed in life. The Guru had given them His Lotus Feet in His Sandals. What was worth asking beyond that? By Baba's grace, both of them were always in a state of bliss. Material things paled to insignificance.

With tears of devotion, Hari and his wife fell at the feet of Baba, praising his compassion and grace. Hari said, "May you be always pleased with us. Give us your blessing that we may always have the bliss of the company of Your Lotus Feet, and have devotion to you. We want nothing but your compassionate blessings to be eternally at your feet." Pleased with their simple devotion, Baba granted the boon of *"Consciously leaving the body at death, in a state of deep meditation of the Brahman, the pure Consciousness."*

Haricharan led a simple life as a householder with a wife and children. With his mind utterly given to God in the form of Baba, he reached a high state of yogic attainment. Sanctified by the constant utterance of his Guru's name, he manifested mystic powers. When he grew old, he understood when his death was approaching. The time for the fruition of the boon of *Kalpataru* Lokenath had come. Three days before his death, he asked his wife and children to leave him alone. In a state of deep meditation, he contemplated the lotus feet of his beloved Baba and left his body in a conscious state according to Baba's blessing. The part merged into the Whole. Haricharan merged into the Cosmic Ocean of Eternal Bliss. Glory to God and all glory to the pure devotee! Haricharan demonstrated simple *Guru-bhakti* and its pure culmination in the deep absorption of enlightenment.

SURATHNATH BRAHMACHARI

Surathnath Brahmachari was a powerful example of Satguru Lokenath's Grace. Before he came to Baba and was fortunate enough to receive spiritual instruction from him, Surathnath lived in a village called Govindapur in the district of Dacca. He was known at that time as Akhil Chandra Sen. Tall, extremely handsome and wealthy, he fell into bad company early and lead a life of vice, addicted to wine and women. This continued for a long time before he reached a turning point.

Tales of the Himalayan mystic of Baradi were in the air everywhere. Hearing them, the desire grew in Akhil Chandra to go to Baradi for Baba's *darshan.* The chance came and he set out for Baradi.

Baba pulled Akhil to his shelter. Meeting a Godman for the first time in his life, Akhil experienced unspeakable inner ecstasy. All his life, he had enjoyed all the physical pleasures, but they were fleeting and frustrating. In the presence of Baba, he had the taste of pleasure beyond the senses. It shot to and from the core of his being. Tasting supra-sensual bliss, he came to Baradi again and again. The impurities of his mind began melting away in Baba's Divine Presence.

Akhil was not only handsome; he was very particular about his dress. He wore only the most modern outfits, with a gold-coated watch. One day, Baba asked him, *"Why have you put on such costly dress?"*

Surathnath Brahmachari

Akhil replied with immediate conviction, "This body is the temple of God. If I don't decorate this, what else am I to decorate?"

Baba was pleased with the answer from his child. He was happy to see that in the midst of body identification there was now an evolution of consciousness toward the purpose of the body.

Gradually, in the presence of Baba, Akhil worked out his accumulated past (*prarabdha*) and came closer and closer to the Guru. Finally, one day Baba called Akhil, gave him spiritual instruction and ochre colored clothes, and initiated him in the order of *Brahmacharya*. Baba renamed him Surathnath Brahmachari.

Touched by the Divine Grace of Satguru Lokenath, Surathnath made quick progress in spiritual practice. Having left all of his old habits and attachments behind, he lost himself in the practice of Guru-bhakti and meditation. He rose to heights of spiritual attainment within a short time to become the instrument of his Guru. Whoever came to him was touched spiritually and healed of all physical and mental ailments. In later life, he initiated many devotees into the path of bhakti (devotion to God and Guru) as a Guru. Honoring the glory of his Master, he said, "Even a beast like me was transformed into gold by the touch of Satguru Lokenath."

Baba teaches all of us a strong lesson through the life of Akhil Chandra. The past, however abhorrent, is not important. The present is all that matters. Akhil, with his sensual background, was not rejected by God. He was accepted with love, given the opportunity to become a saint and to explore the infinite potentialities of being. Most householders with a past suffer from self-condemnation and have a complex regarding their ability to walk the path of spiritual light. But Baba Lokenath, through Akhil, shows us that if we can surrender, the transforming grace of the Satguru will make the impossible possible. At a ripe age, after inspiring many people toward divine life, Surathnath left his body and reached the Ultimate Home of unity with his Master.

KRISHNA CHANDRA ROY

Krishna Chandra had suddenly lost everything and become almost a pauper. He was adrift and without purpose, when he met two Sannyasins who took him to a mountainous region, where he served them while they mediated.

The saints were pleased with Krishna Chandra's service, but said to him, "You must go back to the life of a householder. We see that you will be blessed with two sons. We also see that you will have the good fortune of having the company of a great Master who resides at the bank of river Meghna. He is your Guru. Go to him and you will have the fulfillment of all your desires."

The Guru is destined in the life of a true seeker. The destiny unfolds as time ripens. Against his wish, Krishna Chandra obediently left the sweet company of these saints to assume the role of householder.

He found Baba awaiting his arrival at the bank of the Meghna River. The moment he saw Baba, he surrendered for the rest of his life.

In time, he was blessed with two sons, Haridas and Janakidas. Krishna Chandra spent most of each day in deep meditation on Baba.

To him, Baba was God. After Baba took his mahasamadhi, Krishna Chandra offered his time solely to the worship of Baba's image. He meditated without ceasing. In no time, the grace of the Guru flooded Krishna Chandra and he saw the entire world as the manifestation of Guru Lokenath.

Baba began manifesting his Divine Lila through the body of Krishna Chandra.

People from far and wide began coming to him to fulfill their wishes. People with incurable diseases took shelter under his benign influence and were healed. With Baba's grace, he reached a high state of compassion. Through yogic means, he could attract the disease of others into his body and suffer on their behalf.

Once, a devotee came to Krishna Chandra crying and praying for the life of his son, who was afflicted with an incurable high fever. Realizing the disease was terminal, Krishna Chandra said, "This disease is terminal. There is no way to heal it." The devotee cried bitterly and prayed for the life of his son. Moved by compassion, Krishna Chandra drew the disease into his own body. He then came to his ashram at Dacca and declared that his death was inevitable.

In spite of high fever and intolerable physical pain, he continued preparing food offerings for Baba and performing the rituals of Guru worship. When the time to leave his mortal body was near, he left Dacca and came to the Baradi Ashram of Baba, where he sat in *yogasana* (yogic posture of meditation). He left his body while chanting *"dayal guru! dayal guru!"* ("Oh, Compassionate Guru! Oh, Compassionate Guru!") and merged into the Guru (Cosmic) Consciousness.

JAMINI KUMAR MUKHOPADHAYA

Jamini Kumar Mukhopadhaya was one of Baba's closest devotees. His book on Baba's gospel, entitled *"Dharmasaar Sangraha,"* is one of the most authentic resources on Baba's eternal teachings. While many devotees were fortunate to sit close to the Living Buddha, it was Jamini who recorded the words that poured from Baba's Divine Being. Without the wish and blessings of the Satguru, no one can do that work. Jamini's book was appreciated by people of all faiths.

Jamini first met Vijay Krishna. It was from him that Jamini heard about Baba. Vijay said to Jamini, "Though I have traveled to numerous holy centers in the hills and mountains of India, I have never met a yogi of his stature. In all of India, there is not a person who could be compared to his state. His eyes never blink. Yogis from the Himalayas come to him during the night to take lessons on advanced yoga."

Jamini could hardly believe such a great saint lived so close to his home, or that one who taught the Tibetan and Himalayan yogis in their subtle forms was available to the common people. Without wasting a moment, he rushed to Baradi and was transformed. His whole being was flooded with peace and joy the moment he saw Baba. After deep communion with Baba's presence, he returned home filled.

At home, he said to his Mother, "Mother! You cannot love me as much as Baradi's Brahmachari (Baba)." If anyone asked him about Baba, he would say, "I have seen 'the Living Gita' with my own eyes."

Jamini wrote, "Brahmachari Baba was very practical. He used to say, 'You cannot tell others what you have not experienced yourself.'

In order to explain the role of the Satguru in the life of a seeker, one day after his food, he called me and asked me to sit by his side. Quite unusually, he asked for food again. When food was served the second time, he started to eat. With his own hand, he put food into my mouth. While feeding me, he asked, *'Jamini! What is happening?'* I said, 'You are putting food into my mouth and I am chewing and eating it.' He said, *'The Guru does this much. He puts the food in the mouth. That's all. The disciple has to chew, eat and digest all by himself.'"*

This dramatically enacts the essence of the Guru's role. It portrays the way the Satguru teaches the path to Self-Realization. Baba could have simply instructed Jamini with words. To show how much he loved Jamini, however, he asked for food and ate from the same plate with his disciple, which he never did for anyone else. Baba was making it clear that it is not enough to have a Guru who has reached a high state of spiritual attainment. It is not enough to be in close physical proximity to the Guru. Most important is the sincere effort on the part of the disciple to actually tread, with utmost trust and patience, the path set out by the Guru. The Guru can hold the rudder of the boat to cross the ocean of life; he can provide direction. But he cannot row for the disciple. By living the Guru's teachings, the disciple moves across the great waters, all the while building confidence in the Self, and deepening trust in the Guru.

RAMKUMAR CHAKRABORTY

Born to a Brahmin family of Baradi, Ramkumar manifested the best qualities of life. Once he finished with his duties as a householder, he offered himself totally at the feet of Baba to realize his higher Self.

When the time was ripe, the Guru awakened the spirit of true renunciation and love for God. There are genuine reasons to believe that Ramkumar Chakraborty was no other than Guru Bhagwan. The moment he came to Baba, his dormant longing for renunciation surfaced. He wanted nothing more than to leave home and to perform penance in nature as a wandering mendicant. Baba gave Ramkumar very special attention and instructions on the path of yoga. He also directed him to leave home and become a true sannyasin.

Blessed by Baba, Ramkumar felt his inner prayer being answered. He left home. In parting, Baba said to him, *"Ram, when the time comes, I will call you to me. Whenever you remember me, you will feel my presence with you."*

Years later, he appeared at Baradi with the transformed look of a sage. It was June 1st 1890.

On June 2nd Ramkumar, in the company of an old man from the village, Chandrakumar Bhattacharya, went to have the darshan of his Guru at the ashram. Baba called him inside. Chandra was asked to wait outside. Guru and disciple talked to each other privately for quite some time. Chandrakumar said that he could feel that both of them were in deep spiritual communion. Baba told Ramkumar that he had called Ramkumar from so far away because he had decided to leave his body that day. He instructed Ramkumar to perform all the ceremonial funeral rites in accordance with scriptural injunctions.

Ramkumar performed the last ceremonial rites that day after Baba's mahasamadhi and stayed in the ashram for three or four days. He consoled thousands of devotees who were agonizing over the loss of the Living God. Ramkumar told them, with the light and power of realization, that Baba's death was merely the disappearance of the body, that Baba is eternally vibrant, present, and inseparable from the hearts of his devotees.

Ramkumar left Baradi and went to Varanasi to the Manikarnika Ghat, where he sat in meditation and took his own mahasamadhi. Nishikanta Bose, an ardent devotee of Baba's, wrote in his personal diary how Ramkumar had received the subtle message from Baba to come to Baradi for Baba's mahasamadhi and the subsequent events until Ramkumar's mahasamadhi at Varanasi. Amarchandra Bhattacharya, a close relative of Ramkumar from Vidyakut village of Tripura district, had told the story to Nishikanta.

Opinions were divided as to who among the closest devotees and disciples was Guru Bhagwan. Many claimed it was Brahmananda Bharati. To the followers of Rajani Brahmachari, he was Guru Bhagwan. If we analyze the lives of Baba and Ramkumar, however, telling and mysterious parallels are evident.

Ramkumar was attracted to Baradi by Baba from a great distance away just before Baba's mahasamadhi. Baba gave Ramkumar the final touch of grace for the Ultimate union. Just as Baba performed the last ceremonial rites to his beloved Gurudev, so also, despite the presence of his closest disciples, Baba instructed Ramkumar to perform his last rites.

Guru Bhagwan left his body at the Manikarnika Ghat at Varanasi. Ramkumar traveled all the way to Varanasi from Baradi to take his mahasamadhi at the same place. All these are significant indicators.

In the same diary of Nishikanta Bose we find further corroboration. Nishikanta met one Ramanimohan Das of Narinda village, who narrated the following story.

Ramani's nine-year-old son was saved from certain death by the grace of Baba Lokenath. After the boy regained his health, from time to time he entered spontaneous, trance-like states in which he became a medium of Baba Lokenath, Benimadhav, or Guru Bhagwan. The trances began with the boy saying, "Baba Lokenath has come! Benimadhav has come!" In his normal consciousness, however, he remembered nothing.

Ramani knew nothing about Nishikanta at the time. One day, Baba Lokenath ordered him, through the boy, to meet Nishi. He searched for Nishi and found Nishi's residence in Baradi in accordance with the instructions! Ramani told Nishikanta that once the boy was asked, while Baba was speaking through him, who Guru Bhagwan was in this life. Baba replied through the boy that Guru Bhagwan was born as Ramkumar Chakraborty of Baradi for his last birth and that he came to Baradi for his deliverance.

MATHURAMOHAN CHAKRABORTY

Mathuramohan (photo on page 134) was another of Baba's closest and most earnest devotees. When he was young, he went to Baba to be healed of an intensely painful disease. In the process of being physically healed, he recognized his Guru.

He was the head teacher of the High School at Roail village in Dacca District. He left his job to popularize Aurvedic medicines and started a small factory for manufacturing them. Once, when praying for Baba's blessings on his business venture, Baba blessed him and promised that his wishes for success would be fulfilled. Within a very short period, his Ayurveda medicine factory, known as "Shakti Aushadhalaya," became very popular and he became rich.

Mathuramohan was not drowned in the intoxication of *Maya* that money can bring. He pursued his spiritual practice, surrendering to the Will of Baba and the path of *bhakti*, devotion to Guru. He was an extremely devout Brahmin, who filled the early morning hours with Guru-worship, chanting the glory of Baba Lokenath. Immersed in the teachings of Baba on perfecting Karma Yoga, Mathuramohan established a large temple dedicated to the Living Shiva, Baba Lokenath. Today, "Dacca Lokenath Brahmachari Ashram" on the premises of the Ayurveda factory continues to draw thousands of Lokenath devotees every day.

Mathuramohan sang the glory of his Guru saying, "The world teacher Sri Sri Lokenath Brahmachari Baba was the greatest among the siddha yogis. He was the living illustration of the glory of Brahman as the Knower of Brahman."

Baba often said, *"Descending from the heights of the Himalayas to the planes, I have created a wonderful garden of flowers. In the course of time, flowers will blossom in this garden and the fragrance will spread far and wide."*

The garden is the garden of Baba's grace. The garden is Mother Earth. From time to time, his grace will manifest in the hearts of a chosen few who will become the Pure Field of Energy. They will be the flowers of purity and perfection, selflessness and love. As time advances, the fragrance of Baba's manifested grace will spread far and wide, touching millions, opening their heart centers to the work of creating heaven on earth. You, too, can be that field. Your sincere practice and surrender to Baba could attract the transforming grace and foster the blossoming of the God-seed in you. It happens through your conviction and sincerity, through your constant effort toward the Divine.

Mathuramohan heard Baba say, time and again, *"I am infinitely wealthy,"* and *"My abundant wealth is readily available to my earnest children all over the world."* This is Baba, the Father, whose heart is as vast as the heavens and as deep as the ocean, who freely gives all to his loving children. He extends his fathomless love to us with his promise, *"You will sit at home and enjoy."*

This does not mean Baba's grace will be showered on those who do nothing and who immerse themselves in a tamasic (lower energy), idle life. It signifies that his children, those who sincerely take shelter under his Divine Grace, need not leave the world, renounce everything, move to the ashram or the monastery, or live alone meditating in the mountains. Like Mathuramohan, we can be sincere devotees, very much in the world, without being engrossed in the false identities and vanities of the ego.

Long after Baba's *mahasamadhi*, Mathuramohan had an experience which indicates that even today Baba can manifest in his gross body to a devotee if the call is earnest. Mathuramohan had gone to the Lord Viswanath (Shiva) Temple in Varanasi with a deep, unspoken desire to have the darshan of his beloved master in his physical form in the temple! At the time of the *arati* (lamp offering ceremony) there were too many people at the doors of the Shrine. Unable to enter, Mathuramohan stood at the gate. Suddenly he felt someone pulling him from behind, holding his hands. He turned and saw Baba Lokenath standing there. Before he could absorb the reality of the situation, Baba pulled him through the crowd to the Deity. Seeing Baba coming, everyone moved away. He walked through the gates right up to Lord Shiva along with Mathuramohan.

Mathuramohan dissolved in bliss in the physical presence of Baba before Lord Shiva. He drank in the effulgent form of the Living Shiva and fell at Baba's feet. After the *arati*, Baba pulled Mathuramohan back outside. Then he moved through the dark alleys and disappeared!

At another time, Mathuramohan was looking for a place to live in Varanasi. He was concerned about which house would be most auspicious for him. Sitting outside contemplating that question, he suddenly saw Baba appearing in full form in the sky, with his finger pointing to a specific house, saying, *"Good house."* Needless to say, Mathuramohan bought that house.

JANAKINATH BRAHMACHARI

Janakinath was born the only son of devout Brahmin parents in Baradi. His father, Ramratan Chakraborty, was a popular Ayurveda doctor. Baba took extreme measures to bring this disciple close to him and showered him with boundless Grace.

At a very young age Janaki had an acute attack of Kalaazar, a typically fatal tropical fever. Day after day, treatment by doctors and his father did no good. He was sinking nearer to death every day. Janaki's parents were nearly mad with grief. After all medicines had failed, they realized that only Baba could save the life of their son. Ramratan and his wife carried the stricken young man to Baba's ashram. Weeping, they placed him at the Divine Feet of Baba. Unable to bear the thought of losing his only son, Ramratan prayed, "Baba, without your grace this child cannot live any longer. We know that your Will is final. You alone can give him life. We have come to beg his life from you." Baba calmly and compassionately replied, *"Leave him at the ashram."*

The next day Baba instructed Janaki, *"Go fetch water from the tank at the eastern corner of the ashram and get involved in ashram service."* This simple instruction carried a direct transmission of power which is unique to the Satguru. Inspired and energized, Janaki followed Baba's instructions. Through service, he gradually improved his health. Every day, he took Baba's *charanamritam* (holy water which has washed the feet of the Satguru) and rubbed his body with the dust of Baba's feet. These were his medicines.

Janaki gradually began practicing yoga exercises and meditation under Baba's direct guidance. When the news of Janaki's sound health reached his parents, they came to Baba, asking for permission to take their child back home. Baba asked Janaki to go back home. But the seeds of renunciation had sprouted in the company of the Satguru and now took the upper hand. With humble submission, he surrendered to his master saying, "I had no hope of surviving. It is only through your grace that I received my life back. No one else has any right to this body. This body is meant only to serve you. I have offered it to you only, for your service, worship, and meditation. I will never go back to the life of a householder with family."

Janakinath Brahmachari

Baba looked at Janaki in silence. Janaki's mother broke into tears, further imploring him to come home. Janaki's commitment to dedicate his life to his Guru was unshakable. His resolve to remain a renunciate, serving in the ashram, was so strong that ultimately his mother bowed to it and left Janaki at the feet of his savior for good.

Freed from the obligations of the life of a family man, Janaki dove deep into the ocean of the Guru's grace. With his body, mind, and soul surrendered to God, he experienced deep communion. Practicing the eightfold yoga of Patanjali (Astanga yoga) under the direct instruction of Baba, he quickly rose in the heights of yogic attainment. Continuously serving Baba's physical needs and meditating upon his Divine Form, Janaki's physical body and consciousness gradually changed to the form of his Guru. Baba's Grace flooded his being. Mystic powers flowed out of him spontaneously.

Baba instructed Janaki to assume full responsibility for the ashram after Baba left his body. Janaki was awed. How could he take care of the ashram in the absence of his Guru? Janaki did not realize that, sitting in the ashram of Baradi, he would be an imminent example of true *Guru-bhakti* to other devotees. He would be the next in the ashram to represent the God who walked the earth.

Baba called Janaki to him and asked, *"Are you worried about how you will take care of the large expenses of running the ashram? Do you think I will be dead and gone? I am indestructible. To reassure you, let me tell you, every day when you clean my room you will find two rupees (currencies) under my matspread. That will be enough for the expenses of the day."*

After Baba took his *mahasamadhi,* every day until the last day of Janaki's life, Janaki found two rupees lying under the seat of Baba as a tangible symbol of Baba's blessing and presence in the ashram.

The elderly people of Baradi spoke highly of Janaki's intense love for Baba. When he cooked food offerings for Baba every day, the entire ashram filled with a heavenly fragrance. After Baba's *mahasamadhi,* he continued to cook the daily offering. After offering it to Baba in the temple, he would bring the *prasad* outside, calling, "Come, come." Hearing his call, two jackals and many other birds and animals came running to eat Baba's blessed food from Janaki's hands.

Being completely identified with the Guru, Janaki's body became the instrument through which Baba's yogic powers manifested. After Baba's *mahasamadhi,* seekers and those in distress found refuge in Janaki. Reports of Janaki's compassion and mystic powers spread far and wide. Large numbers of people seeking spiritual guidance came and embraced him as their Guru.

One of Janakinath's disciples, Gurudayal Das, was blessed with a son. From birth, the child was very weak and blind. One day Gurudayal came to the ashram, praying to Guru Janaki for sound health and vision for his only child. Janaki said "Go, take the dust of this ashram and smear it on the body and eyes of the child. Soon he will be healthy and will have vision."

Gurudayal followed the words of his Guru. After a few days the child regained his health and, to the awe of all the villagers, could now see! The blessed child, named Bhagwan Das, lived in good health and with perfect vision for more than 92 years.

Janakinath once gave a one paisa (one cent) coin to a devotee, Trailakyanath, who was very poor, saying, "Keep this coin safely and you will never have poverty in you life." Soon Trailakyanath's economic situation changed for the better. Even his children and grandchildren lived in peace and prosperity!

Haricharan, a fisherman who lived close to the Baradi ashram, had deep faith in Baba Lokenath. Everyday before sunrise he bathed and came to Baba's ashram, prostrating himself in front of Baba's cottage and smearing his body with the dust of Baba's feet. Then he would go about his daily chores.

In his heart he had the secret desire to be accepted as a disciple by Janakinath. Janaki was aware of the simplicity and devotion of this humble devotee. On an auspicious day, Janaki called him and initiated him in the path of Yoga. Haricharan continued to perform all the duties of family life, but his heart and soul were offered to Guru Janaki. His indifference toward everything worldly and the authenticity of his renunciation impressed everyone in the village. He soon came to be called as "Haricharan sadhu" (sadhu means true lover of God). Leaving his mortal body, he sat in meditation consciously chanting the name of Guru Janaki and passed into the eternal realm to meet Baba Lokenath.

Janaki's renunciation and single-pointed devotion transformed his mother, as well. The mother who had once begged for her son to come home followed him into a long life of renunciation. Living within her family as a sannyasini, she wore ochre colored robes and let her hair grow long and matted while she became immersed in the Divine.

Janakinath had come to Baba for his life. Baba fulfilled that wish and initiated him into the deepest secrets of life. The fragrance of Janaki's austerity and *Guru-bhakti* spread to thousands of thirsty souls who took shelter under his Divine guidance.

Janaki Brahmachari took his mahasamadhi in 1912. Later, under the Divine direction of Baba Lokenath, a samadhi temple was built over the mortal remains of Janaki, the embodiment of Guru-bhakti. Along with the regular rituals of worship and food and lamp offerings to Baba in the main temple, the same rituals are offered for Janakinath today. Janaki's samadhi temple, which stands next to Baba's, is a vibrant symbol that the true devotee and God are inseparable.

The devotees described above represent only a few of the innumerable seekers who regularly visited the ashram and received Baba's boundless grace. Baba provided careful guidance to the devotees who surrendered themselves at his lotus feet. He inspired them to follow the path that suited each individually, according to their own nature and karma. The dominant teaching, however, was always according to the example he had set in his relationship with his own beloved Guru Bhagwan: *"Unconditional surrender to the will of the Master and the Supreme Lord."*

These tender, intensely personal expressions of grace flowing from the Satguru's heart into the life of sincere devotees are much more than stories. They mirror the relationship to the Divine for which we most long. They are sources of living, kaleidoscopic light thrown into our hearts across centuries. They stir us with the sweet, pure essence of the Guru-disciple relationship. And they call to us to come back to them, again and again, for a deeper awakening of the qualities of heart and service which we long to lay at the feet of the Divine.

MEDITATION

Go back to a story contained in this chapter which particularly stirred you. Reread it meditatively, feeling the tender possibilities and longings for such qualities of discipleship to flower in your own heart. Imagine your day-to-day life and spiritual practice flowing out of those qualities of discipleship. Then take your longings to fulfill that vision for yourself as a devotee into meditation, asking Baba to perfect those qualities in you. Close your meditation with a few moments in which you open yourself as completely as possible to the unique and unexpected ways the Divine may use to work with you in your spiritual unfoldment.

CHAPTER 13

BABA'S COMPASSION FOR ALL CREATURES

AFTER OBSERVING INCOMPREHENSIBLY arduous penance for nearly a century, Baba reached a state where he occupied a body but was beyond it. His compassion flowed to one and all while spontaneously manifesting the *siddhis* or mystic powers of highest attainment. His love was universal. He was beyond the limitation of the ego, which draws boundaries and thereby creates separation and ignorance. He showered his love impartially upon all. Whenever anyone asked him for a boon, whether spiritual or material, it was granted without the slightest hesitation.

The recipients of his boundless love and compassion were not only human beings of varying caste, color and creed, but also animals and birds and all living creatures. In the impartial eyes Baba, there was no difference between a wealthy devotee offering a basket filled with fruit and a small ant receiving food from him.

He was a benefactor of the highest order because he was above all discrimination and selfish, narrow sectarianism. No one ever left him with empty hands. Even evildoers received their share of Divine Grace and were transformed into responsible members of society.

To the seeker of wealth, Baba gave wealth. To seekers of the spirit, he gave inspiration and guidance. To seekers of knowledge, he gave knowledge. The hungry received food; the unsheltered, shelter. Those dying from incurable diseases who had given up hope found that they were healed. Like Master Jesus, Baba's word alone could heal the sick.

Baba's appearance was misleading. He was often tough and known to speak rudely when the occasion called for it. In reality, he was the deeply compassionate mother whose heart was pierced by her children's suffering, as we see when he said, *"Do you think that I want you to suffer the pain of your diseases? You have accumulated bundles of sins for many births. How else can you get rid of them without your physical ailments and mental agony?*

"When I see the pain of your suffering has become intolerable for you, then I cannot bear to see you suffering any longer. I know very well that by curing you of your ailment I am indirectly encouraging you, but I cannot remain indifferent. I reassure myself by saying that they are my children. Who else but me will cure their painful diseases?

"I will abuse them, punish them, and at the same time take them on my lap. I do not advise anybody, nor do I want to hear anybody advising me. This is the place of command and order, not of advice. I will do that which is right.

"I do not care for any rules or dictums, for I am free. I am free to do that which I think is right."

In this statement, Baba speaks from supreme authority. He is not bound by the laws of nature. He can remove an individual's karma if he is moved to do so. This is a powerful demonstration of Divinity. In that supreme state there is no second. Baba resides in every heart.

ASTASIDDHI —THE EIGHT DIVINE POWERS

In the *Yogashastra,* it is said that the *Siddhas,* the Blessed Ones, are endowed with the eight Divine powers which are called *Astasiddhi.* After attaining Brahmanhood, Baba became the living expression of the *Astasiddhi,* which manifested as spontaneously as fragrance from a flower. These eightfold powers are called *Anima, Laghima, Mahima, Prapti, Prakamya, Ishita, Vashita,* and *Kamavasayita.*

Anima is the power with which a yogi can move about in his subtle body without being seen by others.

Laghima is the power with which the yogi can levitate and become as light as air.

Prapti is the power with which a yogi can manifest any object or create any situation the moment he wishes to do so. This is the power to heal.

Prakamya is the power that enables a yogi to see through an object at a distance.

Mahima allows the yogi to experience the seamless unity of the entire universe and all existence within his own being, and to simultaneously reveal his all pervasive form to others. An example is given in the Bhagavad Gita, when Lord Krishna reveals His all-pervasive form to Arjuna. Baba's gift to Vijay Krishna, who saw the Cosmic manifestation in Baba's body, is yet another example.

Vashita is the power with which the yogi can move about freely, at will.

Kamavasayita is the power with which a yogi can stay or move about freely on earth and in the sky, or on other planets.

Only a fully Divinized body can receive and attain all of these spiritual powers. Through strict disciplines of yoga, the body of the yogi becomes Divinized. The very atoms of the body change. Only in rare cases does an individual reach total Divinity, through the transformation and Divinization of body-mind, vital body and intellect. These eightfold *siddhis* are the result of total Divinity.

Baba Lokenath possessed all of these great powers, but he had no need or desire to demonstrate them. They were spontaneously manifested only through the will of his devotees. Baba had no desire to do anything on his own. He had no separate existence, as do ordinary, individualized souls. Identifying himself only with the Totality of Existence, his Divine Self became active whenever his devotees sought his assistance and grace.

Innumerable manifestations of Baba's Divine powers became legendary during his lifetime. Today, as well, devotees of Baba Lokenath receive his causeless mercy and feel his protective presence. Baba used interesting methods to teach householders and worldly people. The following incident occurred at the Baradi ashram in the presence of Rajani Brahmachari.

ON UNCONDITIONAL GIVING

Kali Charan Poddar, the son of a rich man in Dacca, once visited Baba's ashram. He came with an offering of five litres of milk and was about to place it before the veranda outside of Baba's room. Seeing this, Baba shouted in a harsh tone, *"No! No! That cannot be kept there!"* Bhojleram, an ashram devotee, immediately removed the milk and placed it underneath the veranda. Kali felt terrible. He came to Baba with folded hands, praying for Baba's kind acceptance. Baba said, *"You are the son of a rich family. If you can give the milk along with a container, I can accept it."*

Kali, without understanding the deeper significance of Baba's statement, found an earthen pot for the milk, and again tried to place it on the veranda. Again, Baba shouted from his seat, *"No! No! That cannot be kept there!"* Once again, the milk was removed and placed on the ground. Soon a dog came and started drinking the milk. Seeing this, Kali immediately drove the dog away.

Observing Kali, Baba told him, *"This is the reason that I did not accept your offer of milk. You have offered me the milk. Once offered, you have no say over that milk anymore. What right do you have to drive out the dog belonging to the ashram?"* It is interesting to note that no dog, cat, or any other animal attempted to touch the milk again after Baba had made his point.

This incident reminds us that, to an Enlightened One, there is no discrimination between rich or poor, man or animal, or any other creature. To him, all are the same. All exist within Him.

Baba's reproach of Kali, *"Once you have offered, you have no say over that milk anymore,"* reveals the essential principle of offering. Offering to the Divine is itself a *sadhana*, a spiritual act. Most people, particularly those who are wealthy, believe that the value of an offering lies in the quantity or the amount given. It is not the quantity, but the *bhav*, the intention and devotion with which it is offered, that is important. God does not care about *what* we bring to the altar, but about the love and devotion with which our offering is given.

"You have no say over the milk once it is offered to me," should be understood in perspective. A gift should be free of the attachment of ego. Once given, the recipient should be under no obligation to use the gift. The giver should not feel offended, whether the gift is used, unused, or given away. The moment the act of giving and receiving is complete, the gift is no longer your property. Release it with joy. This is the ideal.

Generally, most offerings cannot be considered acts of worship because they are motivated by ego. The ego wants its reward. A true giver offers the gift unconditionally and is deeply satisfied when it is accepted. What is done with the articles or the money is of no concern to the true benefactor. Worship is complete once the Divine residing in the receiver has accepted the humble offering. Such detached offering brings a manifold return and elevates the giver to a higher plane of consciousness.

God is the complete whole. The Divine demands nothing, because its true nature is transcendental. The Godman, being *'Atmarama,'* and established in the Transcendental Self, similarly expects nothing from anyone. Wishing only to give to devotees, first he empties and then he fills. Whatever is offered to the Divine, is accepted only to return in manifold, thus fulfilling the desires of the devotees. The offerings must be clean and selfless.

BABA'S TENDERNESS WITH ANIMALS

Only one who has attained Oneness with Eternal Truth can love and care, equally and impartially, for all living creatures. Baba's compassion was uncompromising in its equanimity when it came to the welfare of all his children. He could not entertain the thought of even one ant of the ashram remaining unfed. He understood the language of animals and insects and was often found communicating with them in his own, inimitable way.

Everyone, human, animal and insect, enjoyed the same privilege of his Divine concern and care. Baba loved Kalichan, a bull who was a regular visitor to the ashram, as his own child. There were also quite a few dogs in the ashram. Baba took special delight in feeding them milk, sugar, and other deliciously prepared foods from his own hands.

One day, the ashram cat, called 'Adari' (dear one), was frantic. She was running about, helplessly trying to find a place to safely deliver her kittens. Realizing this, Baba called her, took her onto his lap and helped her comfortably deliver the babies.

Whenever Baba would sit to have his food, he would say, *"Come! Come!"* Birds would fly to him from tree branches without the slightest fear and perch themselves on his matted hair or on his lap. Animals hearing his call came running to eat food from his hand. Even insects responded to his call.

He offered sugar or other sweets to ants and would sit there, watching them carry the food off to their nest.

One day a few visitors came to his ashram. Baba was in his room and the door was bolted from the inside. He shouted from the room, *"Do not come. My family is in the room!"* After some time, Baba opened the doors. As the visitors passed through the doorway, they found Baba with his eyes fixed on the last ants marching out of the room. Baba said, *"I did not allow you to come in because I was afraid that you might unknowingly crush the ants, who were busy receiving sugar from me."*

A street dog once took shelter in the ashram. The poor animal was near death. Seeing the dog's intense pain, Gwalini Ma took pity on him and appealed to Baba, "You have been relieving the pains of all the people coming to your shelter. Why not take pity on this dog and do something for it? His pain is intolerable. And it is just as painful for me to see the dog suffering so much near your Lotus Feet."

Moved by the compassion of Gwalini Ma, Baba immediately rose from his seat and went to the dog. He touched the suffering animal's forehead with his finger and permanently healed the dog's pain.

Another example of Baba's equal vision for animals is described by a person who witnessed the following incident.

"Once I visited Baradi and when I reached Baba's room, I found a woman offering a pot full of milk to Baba. Baba accepted the milk and called loudly, *'Come! Come!'* We could not understand whom he was calling. Within a short while, to our utter surprise and panic, a large King Cobra was moving toward Baba. I was sitting in front of Baba and somehow felt within my heart that in his presence I was safe.

"When the deadly snake reached Baba's feet, Baba held it by the hood, and dipped its head into the container of milk. When the snake had its fill and raised its hood after drinking to its heart's content, Baba said, *'Now you can go,'* and the snake, like the most obedient servant, left.

"Baba then took a little of the milk from the container, put it on his tongue and said to me, *'Take this prasad'* (holy offering). When he found me hesitant to take what was the left from the deadly snake, he said, *'Take it. There is nothing to be afraid of.'* Then I took the milk without any fear. I could never have imagined any human being could have such a friendly relationship with a poisonous cobra."

To Baba, no animal was dangerous or deadly, not even a ferocious tiger. Once, a couple of young men wanted to drive Baba out of Baradi because his wide popularity became great obstruction to the growth of the Institution of 'Brahmo Samaj.' One night, they armed themselves with sticks and made their way to the doors of Baba's room. Suddenly, a large tiger appeared. The boys, terribly frightened at the sight of the tiger, screamed and ran into a nearby room. When they looked out through the windows, they saw Baba coming out of his room. They felt confident that the tiger would do the job for them. To their surprise, rather than attacking Baba, the tiger fell flat at his feet like a harmless kitten. Baba caressed the tiger's head and throat, and said, *"Mother, you should not have come to the ashram.*

People frequently visit this place. Therefore, you should go to the jungle. You will get food to eat there." The tigress understood Baba's words, jumped into the darkness of the night, and disappeared.

Seeing this, the boys realized that Baba was a great saint. Ashamed, they went to him, prostrated themselves at his feet, and asked his forgiveness for their evil intentions. Baba took them into his arms. With a kind voice, he admonished them never to risk visiting the ashram at night again.

Baba taught and demonstrated the value of equanimity and its importance in our lives. For peace to become a reality in the world, it must first exist in the heart of each individual. We must view the needs and troubles of others — and those of our fellow creatures as well — with the same concern that we do our own, and then do our best to help and comfort them. If everyone would adopt this attitude, all human conflict and our ecological imbalances would soon be resolved. A new, peaceful social system would emerge based on reverence for life. Compassion, tolerance and selfless service would surround us.

Only one who experiences himself in every object understands the feelings of all. No utopian ideology, none of the so-called 'isms' imposed from without, will ever bring about equality. Political leaders become intoxicated with power and fame. They are ruled by their egos, which split and differentiate. They can never bring about equality. It is only a person of the spirit, an egoless state of mind that truly embodies equality and fraternity. A deep and profound spiritual journey, undertaken by many, is the only solution to our human problems. There is no other answer.

MEDITATION

As you go into meditation, imagine your body as a hollow, open channel through which the sweet, magnetic light of Baba's Divine Compassion pours. With each in-breath, allow yourself to be lifted, ever more gently and completely, into the energy of compassion. With each out-breath, draw the light of compassion down into your body. Let it fill your body; let it saturate every cell. Experience the tenderness of God's compassion for you. Experience your own compassion for all who suffer.

Throughout the day, hold these questions tenderly in your heart: How have I actively expressed compassion in the past? How have I failed to express it? Where do I express compassion in my life today? What new expressions of compassion and generosity do I choose today, with heartfelt gratitude to God for all that I have been given?

CHAPTER 14

THE DIVINE PLAY

As Baba Lokenath sat at the Baradi ashram playing with his devotees, he taught them the way to truth and freedom.

The Divine Play is sacred and beautiful. The Supreme Child plays all roles, demonstrating the infinite qualities of Divine Reality. As Sri Ramakrishna explains it, "There are two aspects of Reality: Nitya and Lila. The Nitya, or the absolute, is the Indivisible Satchidananda and the Lila, or sport, takes myriad forms, such as the Lila as God, the Lila as the devotees, the Lila as man, and Lila as Universe." (Gospel of Sri Ramkrishana, page 289)

Many devotees witnessed Baba's Lilas. Experiencing the joy, wonder and fullness of Baba's Godhead, they left written accounts so that coming generations could share that experience. In the following two chapters we learn more about Baba's superhuman states as we watch the Supreme Child at play.

THE UNWELCOMED GUEST

One devotee repeatedly beseeched Baba to attend a dinner which he had arranged in connection with the last ceremonial rites for his late father. Baba never left his ashram to attend any such social events and usually no one ever insisted that he attend them in person. Devotees were satisfied if Baba blessed their functions. This devotee, however, would not accept that. After much persuasion, Baba promised that he would attend.

On the day of the event the devotee cordially received his guests, but his entire attention was focused on the arrival of his most important guest, Baba Lokenath. Baba's visit would make his home a holy pilgrimage site. Longing to see Baba, the devotee moved about restlessly. After all the guests had arrived, had feasted and, one by one, had left his home, there was still no sign of Baba. That night the devotee was very depressed. He could not believe that Baba would break his promise. He condemned himself, thinking that he must be a sinner, for how could his master fail him?

The next morning he left his responsibilities to depart for the Baradi ashram. When he reached Baba's feet, he prostrated himself and asked, "How is it that you did not come to our house when you had promised that you would visit? I expected you with all my heart."

Baba replied, *"I did go to your house, but you drove me out."* The devotee was shocked. He had been gracious to all of his guests. He could not remember behaving rudely to anyone. So he said, "Baba, how can you say that I drove you out?"

Baba Lokenath responded, *"A dog tried to take some sweets from the storage room. Not once, but three times, you beat the dog with a stick and drove it away."* Baba then showed the devotee the bruises on his body. *"I was the dog. I visited you in the form of a dog. If you cannot recognize me, what am I to do?"*

The Brahmin devotee remembered the incident instantly. He had beaten a dog three times that was trying to eat some sweets from the storeroom. How could he know that Baba would come to his house in the form of a dog? He fell at Baba's feet and asked his forgiveness.

Baba taught his devotees to acknowledge the manifestation of the Divine in every creature and to observe kindness and goodness toward all in the spirit of worship. The devotee had been good and kind to all his guests, but did not offer a few sweets to the dog as a manifestation of his loving Baba.

SURRENDERING, THE GUILTY ARE PARDONED

Baba once helped a villager overcome dishonesty. The person had been arrested for the crime of forgery and was taken to court for prosecution. During his trial, he refused to confess to the crime. After court had adjourned, he went straight to Baradi, and again insisted on his innocence. Baba said, *"Well, you will be released."*

Having received Baba's assurance, the man left the ashram with great relief. An ashram devotee who knew the truth could not tolerate anyone receiving Baba's grace under false pretenses. The devotee called out to the criminal that the original crime he had committed was pardonable, but not the crime of lying to Baba. He warned the visitor to confess to Baba or suffer the consequences.

Shamed by the chastisement, the man returned immediately to ask forgiveness. When he reached Baba, he fell at his feet saying, "I am guilty. By telling you a lie, I have increased the sin of my guilt a hundred times over. Now my conscience is plagues me from within. I have come to your feet to beg you to forgive me." Baba responded, *"If you have truly surrendered to me, can you do as I say?"*

"Yes!" The man answered. Baba advised, *"Then go to the court and confess your guilt in front of the judges. My promise, 'You will be released,' will not go in vain."*

The man went back to court and confessed his guilt. The judges suspected the villager had been coerced into confessing by the opposite party, so the case was referred to a higher bench. Again, he confessed his guilt. The case finally reached the highest court. The devotee was determined to keep his promise. Strengthened by his faith in the promise of Baba, he confessed his guilt before the full bench of judges. The verdict was in favor of Baba's devotee and he received an unconditional release. Baba's promise had come true.

Grateful for his freedom, the man went running to Baradi and prostrated himself before Baba.

Radhika Mohan Roy, a wealthy man of Dacca, suffered from chronic rheumatism which had partially paralyzed him. Though he could afford the best treatments available, nothing improved his condition. His situation seemed hopeless. His wife, a pure hearted devotee, believed that only saints with spiritual powers could help her husband regain his lost health. She made pilgrimages to various places in search of a holy man who could cure her husband. At last, she heard about the Divine powers and mercy of Baba Lokenath and she found her way to Baba's feet.

Radhika Mohan had a multitude of bad habits and disrespected his chaste wife by involving himself in many evil activities. Baba knew the reasons for Radhika's paralytic condition. He was unsympathetic due to Radhika's impenitence and egocentricity. Baba's compassionate heart melted at the tearful prayers of Radhika's wife, whose purity and devotion remained unstained. Though the husband had neglected his wife and was a dissolute character, Baba took pity on him only because of the heartfelt prayers of his virtuous wife.

With Baba's grace, Radhika slowly regained strength in his limbs. After a few days he began to move. The change was considered a miraculous improvement since he had been a total invalid. Only his arm remained paralyzed as before.

One day as Baba was sitting in his room Radhika's wife came to him looking very depressed. When she prostrated herself before Baba, Baba asked her why she looked so pale. She tearfully told Baba that, although she was deeply grateful that Baba's grace had enabled her husband to move about, she was sad because his arm was still paralyzed. She prayed to Baba for mercy.

Hearing Radhika's wife, Baba raised his hand three times saying, *"Go and you will find that your husband is able to raise his hand."*

The wife trusted Baba's word as the cure itself. Fully convinced of her husband's total recovery, she ran to the boat where her husband was lying. To her great happiness, Radhika had been completely cured of his one sided paralysis.

Another, similar record of healing by Baba depicts how the surrender to his will with complete faith and determination manifests miracles spontaneously.

Sitanath Das, a rich man from Calcutta, had given up all hope of living normally after a lengthy paralysis. He proceeded to Baradi with many attendants. When his boat reached the bank of the river near the ashram, an inspiration opened the gates of Baba's grace. Sitanath decided to lie down on the ground beneath the sky in front of Baba's room. He was determined to persist with this penance, which exposed his body to the elements. Sitanath stretched himself on the open ground for two consecutive days.

Family members and servants pleaded with him not to subject himself to so much pain while in such fragile health. But Sitanath was determined to receive Baba's grace through surrender. Even if he were to die, he told them, he would be privileged to die at the feet of a great yogi.

Initially, Baba remained indifferent. He acted as if he were not even aware of Sitanath's presence in the ashram. He was merely testing Sitanath's determination and trust. His grace flowed inevitably to those who had devotion and faith in him. After two days, in the early hours of the dawn, Baba went to Sitanath and called him by name.

When Sitanath saw the unusually tall Baba standing and looking at him compassionately with eyes as wide as lotus leaves, he was deeply moved. Lokenath touched his body, saying, *"I have given you a lot of pain. Now get up."* As if touched by magic, Sitanath immediately felt quite strong. He sat up by himself, then stood on his feet. Overwhelmed with gratitude, he collapsed at Baba's feet in tears. In a moment, he had regained his lost health. He felt so strong and healthy that the memory of his long ailment seemed very faint.

Baba embraced Sitanath and said, *"I am pleased to see the spirit of surrender with which you have been lying under the open sky at the ashram, disregarding your attachment to your body and mind, your wife, children and personal property. I have shed tears for you. Now you are well again. What you have surrendered to me will remain with me. From now on, enjoy your life. I am giving you permission."*

This is a beautiful example of how the tears and pain of the devotee move the heart of God. God, too, sheds tears at the pain of his devotees. Baba gave Sitanath the right to enjoy everything in life with the sense of detachment he experienced during his stay in the ashram.

HEAVEN'S MILK FOR THE DIVINE CHILD

Another example of Baba's mercy is the story of Sri Umaprasanna Nag. A resident of Baradi, Nag was blessed with an infant son, but he had lost his wife in childbirth. There was no one at home to nurse the baby. Umaprasanna's sister, Sindhuvasini Devi was unable to help him.

Faced with the urgency situation, Umaprasanna decided to find a paid woman who could feed the baby. Learning of her brother's intentions, Sindhuvasini went to Baba Lokenath and explained the situation to him. Baba listened patiently, then told Sindhuvasini, *"There is no need for any paid woman. You come sit before me. I will suck your milk."*

Sindhuvasini knew that she was infertile. She had wished with all her heart to be a mother, but her dream had remained unfulfilled. She could not believe her ears. The mother in her rose to receive the greatest boon of her life, to be the mother of God Incarnate.

The infertile woman sat before the Divine Child. The moment Baba put his mouth to her breasts, they filled with milk. Her clothes were drenched. The motherless child had found a mother in Sindhuvasini. Nourished by heaven-sent milk, the baby grew to be a holy child and an ardent devotee of Baba.

Umaprasanna named the child Brahmaprasanna, since the child lived by the blessings of God Incarnate, Lokenath. In later life, Brahmaprasanna settled in Calcutta and established a temple dedicated to Baba Lokenath at Garia.

Another, similar incident occurred when Baba was sitting in his cottage room in the presence of many devotees. An old woman appeared with her daughter and grandson. The old woman placed the baby at Baba's feet and explained her problem. Her daughter had no milk and the baby would not take the cow's milk offered to him. The life of the child was at stake. Only Baba's grace could save her grandson. She requested that Baba suck her daughter's breasts so they would fill with milk. Baba asked, *"Am I to suck the mother's breasts at this old age?"* Then he called the young mother to him. When she removed the clothes above her waist, Baba suckled like a small child. Then he said, *"I had it; now you can go."*

They left the ashram, but soon returned to Baba with the same complaint. The mother still did not have milk in her breasts. Baba nodded that he was aware of this and told the women that there was no cause to worry. They should keep their trust in Baba and the baby would not die. The women obeyed and the boy grew to be hale and hearty.

Rajani Brahmachari happened to be present at the time. Failing to understand the mystery of this Divine Play, he asked Baba about it. Baba explained, *"The milk I sucked from the mother's breasts was very thick and sweet. They would not understand that, so I had to tell them not to worry about the breast milk and to carry on as before, leaving the child to the will of Baba. Seeing the eyes and physical form of the baby, I knew that the child was not ordinary. He was spiritually advanced. He remained blissful most of the time. Whenever anyone is in a state of spiritual bliss, his hunger is naturally reduced. Hence, his mother's milk, which was thick and very sweet, was quite sufficient for him. There was no need for cow's milk, so the child would cry whenever they offered it to him."*

THE BARREN CONCEIVE

Infertile women would often come to Baba, begging to have children through his mercy. Baba took pity on these women, who longed wholeheartedly to have a child, but for some physical reason could not. Baba always blessed them, saying, *"You will be blessed with a child. I shall come to your home as your child."*

Baba would say the same thing to all these women, so most people found it confusing. When they asked Baba to explain, he would say, smiling, *"To you there is the second. But to me, there is nobody else other than me. I have become everything; so who else will be born other than me?"*

A young woman who had suffered a series of stillborn births approached Baba in the company of her mother-in-law. She prayed for Baba's blessings to successfully carry a child. As was always the case, a devotee's tears moved Baba's compassionate heart. He blessed the woman saying, *"Do save one paise (one penny) every day until the date of delivery. When you deliver a healthy child, come and donate that money to the ashram fund. If that is done, the child will not die."* Her husband faithfully put aside a paise everyday in the name of Baba, and a healthy female child was finally born with Baba's blessings.

HONORING OUR PROMISES TO GOD

One of Baba's messages to his devotees concerned the importance of keeping our promises to the enlightened master!

Sri Chandrakumar Dutta of Bicrampur was the deputy magistrate of Dacca. After a prolonged ailment, his wife had lost her ability to speak, take food, and to pass urine or stool. Though she received the finest medical care, her condition continued to deteriorate. Only God could save her.

Chandrakumar brought his wife to Baba and begged for his mercy. Baba said, *"In order to test whether I had attained the state of Brahman, I cured ninety-four dying patients, just by word. Now I do not have such wishes. But if anybody can make me wish, even today he can cure himself."*

Chandrakumar asked how he could make Baba wish. Baba replied, *"Just as you need food to appease your appetite, just as you need to attend to the call of nature to maintain the health of your body, in the same manner, if anyone needs me, he can make me wish and thereby fulfill his desires."*

With this statement to seekers of Divine Grace, Baba suggests the path of bhakti. The true lover of God reaches a state where aspiration for Divine Grace overshadows all demands of material nature. This occurs through single-pointed devotion and trust in the Divine. The love of God becomes the devotee's lifeblood. The prayer of such a devoted soul never goes in vain, because grace flows in a constant stream to those who are totally dependent upon the Divine Will.

The pitiable condition of Chandrakumar's wife touched Baba's heart. She was so modest that she sat before Baba with her entire body wrapped in her saree so that not one inch of her body was exposed. Baba asked her to extend her hand. When she timidly extended her hand, Baba quickly caught hold and pulled. He stretched out his long legs and said, *"Hold them hard!"* She held Baba's legs with the little energy she still had left in her body. Baba then asked Chandrakumar if he could leave his wife at the ashram. Due to a personal problem, he could not leave her. After returning to Dacca, he immediately sent her back to Baba's feet.

The woman stayed for two months at the Baradi ashram. With the grace of Baba and the motherly care of Gwalini Ma, she regained her lost speech and her other problems disappeared. On the day that she was to return to her husband's home, she had the strength to cook an offering to Baba, which she presented with deep gratitude and devotion.

Chandrakumar's wife returned to Dacca with her health restored. Soon after, Chandrakumar was transferred to Barishal. Chadrakumar, however, had promised Baba that he would offer one month's salary of 500 rupees as a donation to the ashram if his wife recovered. Baba reminded him in a personal letter that he should not forget the promise he made and that he should send the amount to the ashram without further delay. Chandrakumar wrote back, saying, "You are a sannyasin. What are you going to do with so much money?" As a result, within a period of one year after Baba's letter to Chandrakumar, his wife once again fell ill with all the previous complications of her ailment.

There is a serious lesson in this Lila. Chandrakumar had freely promised to make a donation of 500 rupees to the ashram if his wife was cured. The plight of the woman so stirred Baba's compassion that he would have cured her with or without the promise, for Baba had no need for money. However, once Chandrakumar had freely made the promise, it became a binding commitment. Chandrakumar deliberately dismissed his responsibility. When Baba reminded him for his own sake, he arrogantly pointed to Baba's vow of renunciation. In so doing, however, he tempted fate. The blessings that he received from Baba were taken from him. Unfortunately, his wife had to suffer the consequences for his foolish actions.

The Enlightened One never cares for money that is offered. He or she has no personal desires. If the devotee attempts to trick the master or breaks a promise, he invites disaster. By deviating from such a promise, one sows the seeds of misery. One must be aware that once a promise is made to any saint, master, or deity of a temple for the fulfillment of any desire, it is a promise that should be kept at any cost.

A similar incident occurred when a villager from Baradi was bitten by a very poisonous snake. Within moments, the man was critically ill. The efforts of the village doctor and of others proved useless. He was dying. As death neared, the family prayed to Baba as they sat in their home. They promised that if their loved one survived, they would offer special worship to Baba. Within minutes, he improved dramatically. The family promptly forgot their promise. They gave more credit to the role of the doctor than to Baba's Grace.

The snake victim went back to his normal life and work shortly thereafter. But the Divine has its own ways of reminding us! Suddenly, he felt pain where he had been bitten. The poison spread rapidly to every part of his body. He became unconscious with intolerable pain. The family was awestruck. How could there be a poisonous reaction without any reason? Then their promise to Baba flashed through their minds.

Convinced that the whole thing happened only because of their insincerity, they ran to the ashram and prostrated to Baba with offerings of flowers and fruits. Within a few moments, villagers came running in with the good news that the man had returned to normal health!

BABA'S OMNISCIENT MOTHERLY LOVE

Two devotees from the Nag family had come to the ashram for Baba's darshan. When they arrived, Baba said lovingly, *"You have come here without taking food from your homes. Stay on and have some Khichri"* (boiled rice and lentils). Then he got up, went to the storeroom himself, and gave rice and pulses to Gwalini Ma for preparation. Everyone present was stunned to see Baba bring enough grain to feed fifty to sixty people when there were only two guests. One of the visiting devotees made fun of Baba's lack of understanding about the amount needed by remarking, *"Who is going to have so much khichri?"*

After the two had eaten, they sought Baba's blessing and permission to leave. Baba said in the exact tone which the devotee had used, *"Who is going to have so much khichri?"* The devotee was embarrassed, but he still wondered why Baba had Gwalini Ma cook so much food.

He did not have long to wait for the answer. The moment he stepped outside the ashram gate, he found more than fifty to sixty people coming to the ashram. From behind, he heard the amused voice of the Omniscient Baba, *"Who is going to have so much khichri?"*

The two devotees now realized that, just as Baba knew that they came to the ashram without food, he also knew that a large number of devotees were on the way and would be hungry after their long journey. Like an affectionate mother, he had the food prepared before the children arrived. There was nothing that was unknown to him, though he was physically present at the Baradi ashram.

BABA CALLS GOSWAMI FROM DEATH

Once Vijay Krishna had gone to Dharbhanga to teach. While there, he suffered a critical attack of pneumonia. Two famous physicians at his bedside had given up hope of recovery and pronounced that his end was near.

Shyamacharan Bakshi, an ardent disciple of Vijay Krishna, learned that his Gurudev, who was his very life, was on his deathbed. He knew that Baba could do what was impossible and that Baba loved

Vijay Krishna, so he wasted no time in running to the Baradi ashram. Sobbing, he prayed to Baba to save the life of his Master.

Baba always loved a devotee who loved his Guru. The profound feeling, with which Shyama begged for the life of his Master, as well as Baba's own deep love for Vijay Krishna, moved him. Still, the playful Lokenath wanted to further test Shyamacharan's devotion and love for his Guru. So Baba asked him, *"What is it that you can do for your Guru?"*

No one in this world who was as dear to his heart as his Gurudev, so Shyama promptly replied, *"I can give my life for my master. Right now, take half of my life span for my Gurudev. Please save him!"*

Baba was moved by Shyama's devotion, but to further test the depth of his love, Baba said, *"If he goes, why worry. I am here to take care of all of you."* Shyamacharan steadfastly and boldly replied, "We don't want you. We want him back at any cost!"

This fearlessness when threatening to insult a Guru is exactly what Baba wanted to see. He was pleased. His body became still. After a while, he returned from *samadhi* and said, *"You have come when the time is finished. What can I do now? I did not see him in his home. The possibility is that he left his mortal body or his Guru must have given him the power to stay away from the body. You can go now. If you receive a telegram by Tuesday, then know for certain that there is nothing to fear. I am going there."*

Baba had gone to Darbhanga in his subtle form to see Vijay, but could not find him there. Baba's was referring to Vijay's body as his home. Either Vijay had left the body or his Guru had given him permission to stay away from the body. Determined to save Vijay under any circumstances, Baba came outside and told all the assembled devotees, *"Until I open the door from inside, nobody should knock on the door or open it."* Baba then bolted the door from the inside on Friday and announced that the news would come on Tuesday.

That day all of Vijay Krishna's family had started on a steamer to Darbhanga from Goaland. Vijay Krishna's son, Yogjivan, was looking at the sky with a heavy heart, repeating of the Divine Name for the life of his father. Suddenly, he called out to all the others, pointing to the sky, "Look! Brahmachari Baba (Baba Lokenath) is going toward Darbhanga. He waved at me and said, *'I am also going to Darbhanga. Do not worry. There is nothing to fear!'*"

Behind the closed doors at the ashram, Baba's body remained without the slightest pulsation of life. In his subtle astral form, he proceeded to Darbhanga, flying through the sky to breathe life into the near-dead body of Vijay.

Baba moved through fire, water, or space effortlessly. When Vijay Krishna's mother, Burothakuran, reached Darbhanga she saw Baba Lokenath sitting at the bedside of Vijay. His non-blinking eyes were fixed on her son.

The disciples and devotees of Vijay at Dhaka anxiously waited for the telegram with news of the recovery of their Guru. They had full faith in Baba's promise. As Baba had promised, on Tuesday a wire arrived with the news of Vijay's good health.

The close relatives of Vijay Krishna at his deathbed reported clearly seeing Brahmachari Baba (Baba Lokenath) sitting near Vijay's head. More than once, Baba lifted Vijay's body to make him sit on the bed. They saw Vijay Krishna try to sit up on the bed twice, only to fall back to the bed unconscious. On the third attempt, he sat up and was totally recovered.

Vijay Krishna Goswami later declared to all his assembled devotees that Baba Lokenath had appeared at his deathbed and had almost physically pulled him by his hands to make him sit up in the bed. Instantaneously, he had regained his lost energy and had felt perfectly fit.

Vijay Krishna, who considered Baba Lokenath the greatest yogi he had ever met, told about Baba's supreme spiritual powers and how he had saved him from death. Vijay Krishna would leave his physical body due to intolerable pain. Baba would compel his soul to re-enter the body again. This happened twice. Finally, when Vijay Krishna desperately left his mortal body with the intention not to re-enter it again, Baba's great spiritual power overcame his wish and forced the soul of Goswami to reenter the body.

As always, Baba's infinite power had responded to the unlimited, selfless devotion of a disciple for his Guru.

Quite in contrast was Baba's response to those who were insincere. We see this when one man came to the ashram with a dramatic display of devotion. When he fell at Baba's feet praying for mercy and blessings, Baba knew he was a hypocrite and that his devotion was artificial. Baba was rude and said, *"You cannot love your own wife, so how can you love me?"* Baba gave him an indifferent look. Feeling foolish and out of place, he left the room.

Baba's words, as always, were significant. Although spoken to a specific individual, their import is universal. Baba always taught that love of God is not possible unless one loves one's own dear ones. How can one please God, who is the All-Pervasive Existence residing in all creation, while disrespecting our fellow human beings and other creatures? Loving a Divine Incarnation and worshiping in temples without first loving our fellow human beings is hypocrisy.

The stepping-stone to Divine Love is empathy for all living creatures. How can we dream of pleasing God and receiving Divine Grace if we cause pain to the Divine residing in the hearts of all other beings?

Baba says first learn to love the people who are nearest to you. Gradually expand this love to all your fellow brothers and sisters. When you cannot hurt the feelings of anyone, when your heart feels the pain of others, then God, who exists in all, is well pleased and you are blessed.

Most regular visitors to the Baradi ashram and the ashram residents who served Baba experienced Baba's supernatural manifestations. Baba would leave his body at will to move about freely wherever and whenever he wished. Then he would re-enter his body. To him, the body was a cage. He was a bird, free to fly in and out.

Whenever he left, his body would simply remain seated in place, leaning back on the wooden plank that you see in his picture, as if in a state of sleep with his eyes wide open. Devotees grew accustomed to this phenomenon. They would say at those times that Baba was temporarily dead. When he was out of his body, his form was lifeless, with no sign of breath or pulse.

Many were curious about this aspect of Baba's Lila. They repeatedly asked Baba about it and what he did while in his subtle body. Although Baba was extremely reluctant to speak about it, he apparently gave the impression that he visited spiritual seekers and observed their progress. When necessary, he gave guidance for rapid spiritual progress in advanced yoga.

Even today, almost one hundred years after Baba's *mahasamadhi*, seekers of Truth on the path of yoga receive Divine Visions of Baba and are blessed with instructions for their spiritual advancement. Anyone wishing to have Baba's darshan and the ray of his unlimited mercy can receive it by praying to Baba with trust and pure devotion. This is the Truth. It shall hold good through posterity. He is a Guru of Gurus, the Jagadguru, the Universal spiritual Master.

BABA KEEPS HIS PROMISE

A successful lawyer in Dacca, Sri Biharilal Mukherjee, was an ardent devotee of Baba. Once when he was traveling by boat and passing through the middle of a river, a furious thunderstorm suddenly arose. In the violent winds, Biharilal's boat was as helpless as a toy vessel. It tossed by the giant waves until it could barely stay afloat. Biharilal and his fellow passengers recognized that the situation was totally beyond the control of the boatman and began preparing for the end.

Helpless, Biharilal suddenly remembered Baba's promise, *"Either in forest or in ocean, whenever you are in danger, remember Me. I will save you."* He realized that only Baba could save him from certain death. Biharilal began praying with all his heart to Baba. The earnest prayers of the devotee reached Baba's ears. Suddenly, the passengers were aware of a Divine Presence on the boat. As if by magic, the boat slowly balanced itself, then reached its destination safely. Although the other passengers did not know the "Doer," Biharilal did. It was the grace of Baba that had saved him and his fellow passengers from untimely death.

Anath Bandhu Mallik was sitting near Baba at Baradi at the time of this crisis. Baba told Anath Bandhu, *"Anath, Bihari's life is at stake. He is praying to me for my grace. I am going to save him."* Baba's body remained in a state of deep trance for some time. Afterward, he returned, saying, *"Maya, the illusive power of Mother Nature, is so strong! I was a little over concerned about Bihari, so at first I could not trace the actual place of his ordeal. First, I went to Dacca. Not finding him there, I went to his house. When he was not there, I went to the place of the furious storm on the river and found him there. I saved him from certain death and the other passengers were saved along with him."*

Some time passed after this incident. One day, Biharilal went to Baradi to pay his respects to Baba. The moment he raised his head after touching Baba's feet, Baba asked him whether he had remembered him strongly in the recent past. The man had been drawn back into the distractions of daily life in the world and had forgotten that Baba had saved his life. He casually told Baba of his desire to have the darshan of his Lotus Feet. Baba reminded him about the danger he had faced during the storm on the river. Biharilal remembered that fateful day. He immediately fell at Baba's feet and then narrated the story to the assembled devotees.

Biharilal's story is not only a testament to the power of Baba's promises and his reliability in keeping them. It also underscores our vulnerability, as devotees, to overlooking and forgetting the Divine Grace at work in our lives. By failing to fully honor the action of grace in our lives, by letting it fall into the invisible background of our consciousness, we short circuit the magnitude of its potential, transforming effect -- not only for our own spirit, but in the life of the world.

A few devotees from Dacca once visited Baba's ashram. After receiving Baba's darshan, they decided to return home on foot. They hesitated because the day was extremely hot. They were apprehensive about facing the relentless midday sun. Baba called them and said, *"Proceed on your way. You will not face the heat of the sun."*

The devotees obeyed Baba's command and set out on foot for Dacca. A short distance from the ashram, a cloud appeared from nowhere to block the heat the sun. Acknowledging this as Baba's grace, they returned to the ashram reporting, "Baba, as you said, a cloud has covered the sun, allowing us to walk comfortably in its cool shade. But we are not totally certain that it was your power that caused this to happen. We have come to ask you how far the cloud will offer us shade and at what point we will see the sun shining as brightly as before."

Baba replied, *"When you reach Dayagunj, near Dacca, you will see the hot sun again."*

The devotees received Baba's blessings and left the ashram again. They walked many miles as the cloud moved with them, keenly aware of Baba's personal blessings in the form of the cool shade that protected them from the sun. As Baba predicted, the cloud disappeared when they reached Dayagunj. The sun returned with its blazing intensity.

Understandably, the miracle astonished the devotees. Profoundly awed by Baba's grace, power, and love, they walked all the way back to Baradi in the scathing heat rather than proceeding home. Arriving at the ashram, they prostrated themselves at Baba's feet. Baba smiled. The devotees expressed their gratitude for the experience Baba had given them. Baba had proven the personal quality of God's love and protection for sincere devotees. He had shown them that he held the secrets of the universe, secrets that could never be understood by the human intellect. With this miracle, Baba had released all doubts clouding their minds, and had given them a glimpse of the infinite power that is hidden in the human soul.

MEDITATION

Make the day an open-eyed meditation, a search for the Divine and where it might be hiding within your circumstances, or in your need for new ways of seeing and responding.

Imagine that God is playing peek-a-boo with you. Look for the Divine sparkling in people's eyes, shining from their hearts. Feel for it behind their words, driving their efforts, beneath all fear and limitation, discovery and laughter. Open your heart to the deeper, pure light within those around you. Acknowledge the beauty you see in them inwardly and then out loud, so that they know the deeper good in them is seen and responded to.

Do the same with yourself. If you encounter difficulties, observe kindness toward yourself and others. Make every effort to bring forth a higher good, with a spirit of worship and delight.

CHAPTER 15

THE OMNIPOTENT AND OMNISCIENT BABA

THE REALM OF the spirit is beyond the human intellect. Rationalists, who are identified with the intellect, are naturally threatened by things of the spirit. While misgivings about religion are understandable in light of the abuses perpetrated throughout time in the name of God, which does not obviate the truth that spirit, as the ground of all being, holds the secrets of the Cosmos. It holds the key to the mysteries of Nature itself and to our own nature. The mind, intellect, and all material human knowledge, however advanced, pale to insignificance before the ultimate science of life, the science of the spirit.

The life of the spirit and spiritual practice are properly viewed as research. The seeker continuously conducts personal research in the laboratory of his or her body, mind, and intellect. The success of this research earns the seeker the attainment of *siddhi*, enlightenment, the knowledge of the secret of existence.

This knowledge is not objective, however. It is subjective realization. It is being and becoming. As researchers we do not discover anything new. We come to recognize that which has always existed, the Oneness of all Being. This recognition is the state of Realization.

With Realization comes the manifestation of the highest Divine ideals and powers. The Knower of Absolute Reality has been recognized throughout time as the embodiment of Divine ideals, principles and powers. In time, even the greatest, most valiant political leaders are barely remembered. Jesus, Mohammed, Buddha and Krishna, however, continue to be worshipped by billions of people throughout the world.

As we continue with accounts of Baba's lilas, we see further examples of both his unlimited power and deep compassion for all living creatures.

COMMAND OVER THE CELESTIAL POWER

One day while Baba was sitting outside his room, he saw a woman dressed in a red saree standing by his side. The face of the woman was pockmarked. Baba recognized her as none other than Sitala Devi, the demigoddess (celestial being) who is the harbinger of smallpox. Sitala Devi said to Baba, "I want to leave this place." Both of them remained silent. After some time passed, the goddess stepped in front of Baba.

Baba reproved her in a very serious tone, *"I am here. Do you think I am nothing?"*

The goddess immediately stepped back, pleading, "Will you not allow me to leave this place? Am I to remain imprisoned here?" Baba replied to her, *"No, you need not stay here. Just take the route of the lower bank of the river Chawal Baghini. Under no circumstances should you go over the plains where there is human habitation."*

A few days after this incident a family living on the lower bank of the river experienced a severe attack of smallpox. When they came to Baba and reported the smallpox, Baba inquired about the location of their hut and was informed that it was on the lower bank of the river. Baba advised them to leave the hut immediately and run to a place of safety. They were the only family living on the route which Baba had instructed Sitala Devi to take when she left Baradi.

This incident demonstrates Baba's command over celestial beings. Even demigods and goddesses obeyed his command. It should be noted that since that time there has not been any epidemic of smallpox in that area. Every year prior to Baba's coming to Baradi, however, a virulent outbreak of smallpox had swept the area. The epidemics had often claimed the lives of hundreds, even thousands, of innocent villagers.

An individual reaching the state of Absolute Brahman enjoys supremacy not only over ordinary mortals, but also over all the demigods and goddesses of the celestial plane. Vijay Krishna Goswami's vision of all the gods and goddesses in the body of Baba Lokenath also indicates that celestial beings cherish the Presence of one who, in the human body, has achieved the highest state of attainment, the state of Brahman.

BABA AS EYE WITNESS

Baba once had to present himself at a court of law to stand as a witness. Seeing that Baba was an old man, the lawyer for the opposition sought to make that an issue. The lawyer asked Baba his age. Baba replied, *"150 or 155."* The judge did not believe that anyone could live to that age and said, "This is a court of law and such an absurd statement will not be accepted from the witness!"

The lawyer then proceeded with his cross-examination. He asked Baba if he had seen the incident in question. Baba nodded yes. The lawyer challenged Baba's eyesight by asking Baba how he could possibly see from such a great distance. Instead of answering the question directly, Baba demonstrated the Divine power of a yogi. He called the lawyer over and pointed to a tree which stood some distance from the courthouse. Baba asked him whether he could see any creatures crawling up and down the tree. The lawyer, with his ordinary vision, could see the tree but nothing more, so he answered no.

Baba said, *"You people call yourself young, but have such poor eyesight. From here, I can see a row of ants moving up the tree from the ground."*

The case was interesting and had drawn many people. Hearing Baba's statement, many of those assembled in the courthouse rushed out to inspect the tree. Much to their amazement, they saw that ants were indeed moving up the tree from the ground level.

BABA'S ONLY PICTURE!

Rajendra Naryan Raibahadur, the King of Bhawal, felt a deep urge to see Baba with his own eyes. One day he set off for Baradi with all the important members of his cabinet. During the journey, some expressed a difference of opinion on the issue of prostrating before Baba. The King felt that since the caste of the sannyasin was unknown, they would not prostrate before the saint. When they reached the doors of

Baba's room, they saw him sitting in his *Gomukhasana* posture with eyes like lotus leaves. The pupils of his non-blinking eyes were as brilliant as diamonds. The visitors were moved beyond words.

It was the King who first prostrated himself before Baba and prayed for his blessings. Baba smiled and said, *"Did you not make up your minds not to prostrate?"* The King and his men were dismayed to hear Baba repeat the words they had spoken during their journey. They lowered their heads in shame.

Although seated in Divine Silence, Baba drew a broad range of people without the slightest of effort. Even the *sadhus* and *sannyasins* who visited the Baradi ashram would be so overcome by Baba's Divine Presence that they would prostrate themselves and seek Baba's blessing like other householder visitors. Such was the degree of Baba's spiritual influence, not only among common people and royalty, but also among renounced monks.

The King of Bhawal subsequently became one of the most devoted followers of Baba. He began worshipping Baba as 'The Living Shiva.' He always sought Baba's guidance for both personal problems and delicate matters concerning the management of his large estate. The King accepted Baba's words of guidance as final.

The King was determined to take Baba to live on his own estate. He wanted to construct a temple dedicated to 'The Living Shiva,' Baba Lokenath. He continually prayed to Baba to leave Baradi and move to his estate. But it was Baradi that had been chosen by Divine Design to manifest the Divine Play of this Living God. Baba indirectly replied, *"I am everywhere."*

The devotees of Baba Lokenath will remain forever grateful to the King of Bhawal, for it was his interest and sincere effort which persuaded Baba to allow the photographer to take his photo. One day the King arrived at the ashram with a camera loaded on his elephant's back. He expressed his desire to take Baba's photograph, since up to that time none had been taken.

Voicing his usual stand against any publicity, Baba refused. He said to the King, *"This body is transient. What is the use of keeping a photograph of this mortal body?"* The King would not yield easily. He prayed again to Baba, asking for his kind permission, and pleading that he had come with the big instruments of photography such a long distance.

Baba asked, *"How do you think this photo is going to help people?"* The King replied, "Those who will keep your photograph in their homes will find that their homes become temples. Your presence in the photo will always do good to people for all time to come."

When Baba heard how much good the photo would do, he immediately agreed and came out of his room. This was the only time that Baba allowed someone to take his photograph. All subsequent portraits of Baba were inspired by this single photograph.

NATURE OBEYS BABA!

On another occasion, the King visited the ashram with a large number of his followers. When it came time for him to depart, Baba asked him to wait. The King, anxious to go, did not heed Baba's words and started on his journey. The moment he reached the outskirts of the ashram, it began to rain heavily. The King reluctantly returned to the ashram with his associates. As he approached Baba, Baba asked, *"How is it that you have come back?"* The King replied, "The thunder storm forced me to return." Baba casually remarked, *"You have done well."*

When the rain stopped, the King left a second time. Again, he was forced to return because of threatening rains. When his attempts to leave repeatedly failed, he had to consider the reason. He readily guessed that the storms were caused by Baba to teach him a lesson. He finally retreated to the ashram and surrendered at the feet of Baba praying, "I now understand that until you permit me to go, I have no power to leave. I beg your forgiveness for my disobedience. Please pardon me and permit us to go."

Baba smiled and said, *"Well, did I not tell you to wait for sometime and then go? It was because you did not obey my words that you had to suffer the rains. Now you can go."*

King Rajendra Narayan Raibahadur touched Baba's feet and with Baba's blessings left the ashram. This time, the sky was clear with no trace of the rain that had fallen only a few minutes before!

BABA MANIFESTS TO AN AMERICAN WOMAN

Baba's Divine Play was not confined to India. People residing in other countries of the world received Baba's grace while he tirelessly attended to the desires of the people coming to the ashram at Baradi. The following episode was told by one of Baba's devotees. It illustrates how Baba would bi-locate when he heard the call for help.

Dr. Nishikanta Basu, an ardent devotee of Baba's, was a practicing physician in a sanatorium in Chicago. The following is taken from the personal diary of Dr. Nishikanta Basu.

"It was early morning and a patient of our sanatorium came to my chamber to see me and took a chair in front of me. She had come for the treatment of a tumor on her stomach. The condition of the tumor was so serious that she was very much worried.

"Finding me alone, she confided, 'Dr. Basu, I trust you. I have been staying in this hospital for a long time, but without any improvement. What should I do? Whatever you advise me to do, I shall do.'

"I was about to give my reply, when she cried out, 'Stop, don't talk! I see somebody behind you towering above your head. Do you know who he is? He must be your spiritual guide. He has all his hair pulled up on his head. His face is in one direction, and his eyes are looking in another. (Note his eyes.) He has a long, white beard and whiskers. A piece of cloth is wrapped around his body from below the right armpit and having gone round the front, covers the left shoulder. I can see him down to his waist.'"

After this miraculous vision of the American woman, Dr. Basu wrote in his diary: "I did not look behind me, but only kept looking at the lady and knew that Baba had come. He made it clear to me that he is the Divine Presence and he is always behind me protecting me."

"It was Baba's gift of Grace. His Lila inspired in me more love and devotion for him. I remain ever grateful to him for the rest of my life. I was blessed. My human life is fulfilled. I had the shelter of the Omnipotent Lord, my Master. I wrote on a piece of paper, 'Sri Lokenath' and handed it to the American lady. I told her to repeat Baba's name and remember Him. I also advised her to go to another hospital to have her tumor operation while knowing full well that if she went to another hospital, from the business point of view, the sanatorium would lose. Still I advised her to go, because as I was just about to ask her to remain in the sanatorium for a few more days to satisfy the hospital officials, Baba Lokenath appeared to show me the path of truth and forthrightness. By his Divine Presence, Baba inspired me to have the strong faith that He would always look out for me and save me from all dangers. My mind was spontaneously attracted more and more toward the compassionate Master Baba Lokenath."

Once some visitors came to Baradi and stayed in the ashram for a few days. After their blissful stay, they asked Baba for his permission to leave. Baba asked them whether they could delay their departure for a few more days. The visitors explained their difficulties and asked again for his blessings to leave.

Baba gave his permission to all but one, whom he asked to stay behind at the ashram. The devotees understood that there must be some deep significance in Baba's action, so they left the person in the ashram and proceeded on their way.

The visitor who was asked to stay started feeling ill and shortly began vomiting. The sudden illness was a severe attack of cholera. The grace of Baba, combined with the motherly care of Gwalini Ma, saved the person from death. The devotees realized that if it had not been for Baba's grace, they would have left with their ill companion, with possibly fatal consequences.

Once one of Baba's devotees who had a desire fulfilled through the grace of the Mother Kali left some articles with Gwalini Ma to be offered to the Divine Mother. Gwalini Ma wanted to send the offering with some devotees who were to leave for Kalighat. Baba heard the request and said very patiently, *"You can give me the money as well as the things for the offering. You need not send them to Calcutta. I am Mother Kali of Kalighat."*

Gwalini Ma had immense faith in the words of Baba, so without any further question, she left the room to get the articles she would offer to him. On re-entering room, she had a vision of Mother Kali of Kalighat in Baba's seat. In the next moment, she saw Baba on the same seat with a meaningful smile in his face. Gwalini Ma, directly experienced Baradi and Kalighat as one and the same. She experienced Baba as the Whole and as Baba. He is Brahman. He is Krishna. He is Kali. He is total Divinity in human form.

BABA DEMONSTRATES LAGHIMA!

Baba rarely demonstrated his spiritual powers, but one day he delighted one of his most ardent devotees by using the power of *laghima,* a power which enables a yogi to become as light as air.

A middle-aged woman known as Annada Sundari Dasi often visited the Baradi ashram. She was deeply attached to Baba. She had *'vatsalyabhav,'* the motherly feeling toward the Godman. In her eyes, Lokenath was the dearest child of her life. She could not think of anyone other than this old man as her only child and ultimate refuge.

Baba loved this woman deeply and addressed her as mother. One day, the child had a playful wish to sit on the lap of his mother. He said playfully, *"You are my mother. Can't you take me on your lap?"*

Annada Sundari very innocently confessed that because Baba had such a tall body she doubted that she could bear the load of such a big child. "But if Baba gives the power, then of course, it is possible." Baba approached her and sat on her lap. Annada Sundari had a unique experience. Lokenath's large physical body was as light as a feather. Motherly love and devotion poured through Annada Sundari's heart, as she was flooded with devotional ecstasy. Profuse tears streamed down her cheeks and she prayed to Lokenath, "If you wish, everything is possible in this world. You are the Living God, Gopala Krishna."

MEDITATION

Sitting comfortably erect for meditation, with eyes closed, draw the breath slowly in, deeply relaxing with each breath. Observing the energy rising through your body with each in-breath. Imagine the breath culminating in your forehead, at the high altar of Divine Omniscience and Omnipotence. Offer all that you are into the rising light within the breath, utterly surrendering yourself at the high altar. Draw its grace down into your fully relaxed and open body with each out-breath. Lose yourself in the energies of the high altar. Before you close your meditation, imagine those energies flowing out through your heart to all the world, blessing every heart, uplifting every life, healing every ill.

Then thank God, Baba, your Guru if you have one, for all the beauty and grace in your life.

CHAPTER 16

THE UNIVERSAL TEACHER

WHETHER GOD EXISTS or not may be an external ontological question. The living Buddhas who have walked the earth, however, have demonstrated the reality of the egoless state. They have demonstrated too that it is only the egoless, unified being that can lead individuals, society, and the world to any abiding happiness.

If God is love, the Buddhas have manifested love in its sublime purity. If God is bliss, they have lived the most active lives working for the good of humanity while their consciousness and existence springs directly from ecstasy. If God is knowledge, they have stood as living examples of the Omniscient Self, kindling the light of the knowledge that leads to love and bliss in all human beings.

Even if all religion and the idea of God were to disappear from the earth, the world would be transformed if human beings accepted the glorious example and teachings of the living Buddhas.

The flowering of Enlightenment, however, expresses itself uniquely. Just as not two flowers are alike, no two Enlightened Ones are the same. Each is unique, without artificiality. All knowledge and ignorance are transcended, ever absorbed in the blissful, egoless state of Sat-Chit-Ananda, Existence-Knowledge-Bliss Absolute. Their lives and teachings flow in a creative stream from their infinite being, a freshly appropriate revelation to the individual, the moment, the age and to all time, all at once, forever. The Buddhas, their lives and interactions, their teachings, offer us living, mythic images which contain and reflect the whole within us, and release the energy necessary for the evolutionary movement of our own souls.

One day when Baba was seated on the raised platform under the bael tree, the teacher was visited by a pundit from the local school. This person had accumulated vast information from books and proceeded to lecture Baba on the shastras. Baba listened quietly. While the pundit was talking, a crow began making an unpleasant sound, which the pundit soon found intolerable. He threw a stone to make the crow fly away only to have the bird return immediately to the same branch. The crow resumed its noise making. The bird was freely expressing the beauty of its existence through its own sound. When for the second time the pundit attempted to drive it away, Baba interfered.

"You have driven away the crow because the sound seemed very unpleasant to your ears, but your sound, too, seems to me equally unpleasant and disturbing."

The pundit was shocked. How could a crow and a human be considered on the same level? A crow is a crow and man is the master superior to all creatures.

However, to Baba each and every creation is itself the very manifestation of Divinity. He felt the same about the smallest ant as the highest being. For him, the possibility of the ego drawing a line of demarcation had totally disappeared. That had no place in his heart.

The pundit heard only the physical hoarseness of the crow's call and so its sound irritated him. But Baba saw the divine in the crow and heard the sound of divinity in it just as he saw the presence of the divine in the pundit. The all-merciful Baba loathed nothing.

Baba Lokenath was the teacher, the leader, the reformer of the highest order because all barriers of diversity had disappeared in him. He could only see good and do good. Through this episode with the pundit, Baba wanted to teach that nothing in this entire creation should be looked down upon. Each created thing in this world is great in itself.

By respecting others we only respect ourselves. The entire world is a mirror in which we see the reflections of our actions and thoughts. Love begets love. Hate begets hate. Fear begets fear. We see the world, interpret the world, respond to the world, through the distilled essence of our own consciousness, and draw from the world that same essence.

People from all walks of life came to Baba for guidance not only in matters relating to spirituality but also on issues relating to the best way to solve the complex problems of daily life. Baba always showed deep interest in their problems and suggested appropriate action. His suggestions always proved a blessing both to the seeker and to the society at large. Baba advocated mutual respect among all classes as well as interdependence among them without exploitation of any class. Baba wished for *"a social system where love rules and not hate and discriminations."*

A devotee once asked "What is the right path to live a happy and peaceful life?" Baba spontaneously replied, *"Do whatever you like, but do it consciously, with a sense of awareness."* The questioner, however, wanted further explanation and continued, "If you give me permission to do as I please, then what would you say if I hit somebody's head with a stick?"

Baba smiled and replied, *"Do it and see. I asked you to perform all actions consciously. Once you become conscious and aware, you will find that your conscience will prevent you from doing harm to yourself or others."* Evils in society are perpetrated because awareness is absent. All evil actions are the result of unconsciousness. If a person becomes fully conscious of anger and its consequences, anger can no longer cast its evil spell either on that person or on the people around him.

Sin is committed in a state of ignorance and unconsciousness. Baba says, *"The action which brings you a sense of repentance after it is done is a sin, for it throws you into unhappiness. Any action which helps you have more confidence on yourself and creates a happy state of mind is a virtue."* However, Baba says sin and virtue are relative terms; the attitude of mind is the important factor. The consequence of vice is always unhappiness and that of virtue is happiness.

To seekers of truth and bliss, Baba gave instruction. *"If you intend to become spiritual, you must analyze your actions and thoughts each day before you go to bed at night. You must assess the good actions and the evil actions and come to a firm resolution not to repeat evil actions anymore."*

A seeker should try to perform all activities in state of awareness. This is the most important spiritual practice for the spiritual aspirant. Most recurring actions that flow from lust, anger, greed, jealousy and the like manifest only in a state of unawareness. The seeds of these evil tendencies lie dormant in the subconscious layers of the mind.

Nevertheless, Baba says that unless you take the path of "Vichara," the path of conscious discrimination of action and thought, you cannot reach the state of desirelessness. It is only a desireless mind which can take the aspirant to the state of Samadhi. All the sources of the mind's distortion must first be recognized. Then conscious recognition itself will be the remedy for the disease.

Baba also teaches, *"Be angry, but do not become blind with anger."* Do not allow the anger to possess and make you blind, to render you unconscious. It is only when anger is given free rein that it bursts out and causes damage, not only to the person toward whom the anger is directed but also, and more seriously, to the angry person at all levels of being.

Let anger become conscious. Step back, be a witness to anger and its mechanism, to what is appropriate and inappropriate in the situation. The show of appropriate anger in daily life may be inevitable. The father chastising his child, the teacher reprimanding the student, may call out a display of anger in protective guidance of the child. Neither father nor teacher should be consumed by anger. Rather, they should remain a vehicle of appropriate and conscious expression of anger. In this way, anger cannot possess them or damage their mind or body.

Sri Ramakrishna Paramhamsa narrated a beautiful anecdote about anger. Once there were some boys herding cows in a field. A venomous snake lived in the same field. Everyone was very careful not to go near that area. One day a holy man was passing by. The boys came running toward him and cautioned him not to go in the direction of the snake. The holy man said to them. " I am not afraid of that snake because I know the mantra." The holy man began repeating it and proceeded on his way, but the boys were too afraid to accompany him.

Suddenly, the snake rushed out at him. Immediately the holy man started chanting the mantra. The snake lost its power and sat like a worm at his feet.

The holy man said to the snake, "My son, why are you so jealous of others? Let me give you a mantra. By chanting this mantra you will find God within yourself. That will help you not to indulge in jealous activities. So the holy man initiated the snake with the mantra. After receiving it, the snake bowed to the holy man and asked him how to perform these transcendental disciplines. The holy man replied, "Chant the mantra and do not be jealous of others." After saying this, he departed and assured the snake of his return soon.

The days passed by. The cowherd boys observed that the snake did not come after them to strike them. They threw stones at it, but the snake did not get angry anymore. One day one of the boys held it by the tail and swirled it around up in the air and banged it repeatedly on the ground. The snake started to vomit blood and lay unconscious. The boys went home assuming the snake was dead.

Late at night the snake regained consciousness. Very slowly and painfully it returned to its hole. Severely battered, it did not have enough strength to move. After many days, when it could not resist its hunger any longer, it ventured out in search of food, afraid. It ways envious of none since being initiated by the holy man and somehow it was able to cling to its life by eating leaves and fallen fruit.

About a year later the holy man returned to the same place and looked for the snake. The cowherd boys told him that the snake was dead. The holy man did not believe them. He kept calling the snake by its name near the place where he had seen it last. The snake quickly came out of its hole after hearing its master's voice and bowed to him. The holy man asked, " How are you?" The snake replied, "Sir, I am alright." The holy man asked, "Why do you look so thin?" The snake replied, "You advised me not to be jealous of others. So now I subsist by eating leaves and fallen fruits. Because of this I look thin."

The snake had so transformed itself that it no longer possessed any anger. It has almost forgotten that the boys planned to kill it. The holy man said no one could possibly change to such a state by fasting only, so he asked, "What are the other reasons behind your transformation?" The snake remembered the tortures inflicted by the cowherd boys. It replied, "Master, now I remember. The cowherd boys tortured me. They are simply ignorant. They do not know my mental condition. How do they know that now I could not strike nor hurt anybody?"

The holy man replied, "I told you not to bite but that does not mean that you will not try to save yourself. Why didn't you pretend to strike? It is necessary to show anger toward wicked people by assuming a striking position; otherwise, they might hurt you. Just never pour venom into them."

The appropriate expression of anger is what Baba advises. In an unconscious state of mind anger possesses us. We become anger itself. We become blind with anger. Our blindness allows the unconscious to dominate. A person blind with anger commits the worst crimes, then suffers dire consequences. There is little difference between an uncontrolled angry person and a beast.

Baba says that if you want to be blissful, practice awareness. Do not surrender to the bestial instincts within you. For example, a yogi is one who puts forth all his efforts toward waking from the slumber of ignorance and unconsciousness.

As a world teacher, Baba always followed the maxim, *"First practice yourself, and then preach."* He would often repeat this principle to his devotees, a principle he faithfully followed. For example, Baba taught the path of desireless action and the importance of self-help as a virtue to be followed by every individual regardless of material attainment. When local landowners presented Baba the land for construction of the ashram and explained their intention to donate funds to hire laborers to build the cottage, Baba objected. With the help of the local villagers, Baba worked on the construction of his small cottage. By his action Baba inspired the people never to feel ashamed to do menial work since all work is service to the Divine.

After the ashram of Baradi was built, it became a holy pilgrimage site where ideologically conflicting communities of Hindus and Muslims met. The Mohammaden devotees of Baba often visited the ashram and presented their personal problems, both material and spiritual. On issues regarding disputes with the rival Hindu community, Baba's decision and influence always reigned supreme. The word of Baba was the word of God to them. As a sign of their highest respect to Baba, the Muslim community gave up slaughtering cows at Baradi. This decision was softly prompted by the pure influence of the Enlightened One.

On one occasion a devotee came to Baba with a pressing doubt. He doubted the genuineness of the mantra that his Guru had given him. He was hesitant to ask the question and stood mute before Baba. Baba became serious and with a commanding tone said, *"A disciple is not supposed to judge the genuineness of the mantra given by his Guru. Whatever mantra the Guru has given, the disciple should accept and do the japa with devotion and trust."* The clouds which had gathered in the mind of the devotee vanished instantly. He fell at Baba's feet asking for forgiveness and mercy.

This instruction should clear away similar doubts of all seekers and inspire them to have steadfast devotion and love toward the master and his/her instruction. Worldly minded people motivated by material gain may take initiation from the Guru, but when they find that their objectives are not fulfilled, they start disbelieving in the powers of the Guru as well as in the genuineness of the mantra given them.

Baba states straightforwardly, *"Once you accept anyone as your Guru, then surrender with unquestioning faith and 'Mantramulam Guror Vakyam' should be the attitude."* This refers to the Guru Gita, 'The word of the Guru should be revered as the mantra." Before accepting anybody as Guru, the disciple may test the teacher, as it happened in the lives of Paramhansa Sri Ramakrishna and Swami Vivekananda. Vivekananda, with his analytical and logical mind, would not accept Sri Ramakrishna easily, so he tried different techniques to test the genuineness of the master. After Vivekananda became totally convinced, he surrendered unconditionally at the master's feet and remained his humble servant throughout his life.

Sri Ramakrishna used to say. "Before accepting the Guru, see him well during the day and in the night for one year, and once you are convinced about his Divinity, surrender unquestioningly." While seeking a Guru, the disciple should rigorously examine the sincerity of his motives as well as the earnestness of his surrender to the master, and under no circumstances should he judge the Guru. If one has no shraddha (trust) in one's own Guru, there is never the possibility of spiritual awakening and fulfillment.

Baba always attached great importance to shraddha (trust) in the disciplined path of yoga. Baba said, *"Right action, listening to the words of the Holy Ones, and performance of those actions in society which are dear to the Guru is the true Guru seva or service to the Master."*

Baba explained further. *"In an egoless state of mind, the Mind itself becomes the Guru of the spiritual seeker. Pure intellect awakens. The discrimination between the eternal and the transient occurs. If you can achieve the sweet blending of Jnana and Bhakti in your path to spiritual awakening, then shraddha (trust in Guru's word's) will become your shelter, Shraddha will become your friend and path to self-realization."* Baba's utmost trust in his own master is the proof of the maxim, *"Practice first before you preach."*

When Baba did teach, his methods were never predictable. For example, one day a neatly dressed young man walked into Baba's room. Under pressure by his mother, he had been forced to come to Baba, but his rational mind had no room for trust in the saints. Before he could speak, Baba broke the silence of the room with his commanding voice, *"How is it that you have come to meet a cheat, a bogus?"*

The young man was shocked, for he had uttered these very words about Baba when his mother had insisted upon his coming to the Baradi ashram. He stood silently with downcast eyes, utterly ashamed to face Baba.

Baba softened the next moment and said, *"Whoever willingly or unwillingly follows the words of his mother, he is always blessed by God. The prayer of your mother will not go in vain. You have already been selected by the Selection Board. You could have gotten your name in the first list except for the Anthropology paper for which you got a lower mark. You have not cared to know who put the book by Thompson in your study on the night before your examination with three questions marked in red ink."*

Then Baba insisted that the young man open a letter he was carrying to find news about his selection. The young man had received some letters before coming but had not taken the time to read any. He opened one to find the news he had so desired.

Baba said, *"Now do you still take pride in your little intelligence? Do you call this person a bogus?"* He then continued. *"Take a little earth from under the bael tree and rub it on the abdomen of your mother. Her chronic gastric pain will be cured."*

The young man had never felt more embarrassed. He almost collapsed in a state of utter dismay. Baba could feel the young man's turmoil and so his motherly compassion manifested spontaneously. He called the boy in most loving tone and asked him to sit by his side. The young man approached Baba with his eyes filled with tears. He fell at Baba's feet. Baba lifted him as his own child and embraced him with warm, motherly affection, saying *"You have judged me with the intelligence you have, so there is nothing wrong. If there is any fault, it is not yours; it is mine. I have been protecting you for a long time."*

Then Baba cited two instances where the young man had almost met death. Once it was at the hands of a few ruffians, and the other was when his boat had capsized in mid-river. Both times it was Baba who had saved him. Baba continued. *"This is my first and last meeting with you. Now you will start your career in life and after years of active service, you will be posted as the supreme authority of this district. Do not get drunk with power. I wish you to take the responsibility of raising the standard of life in the poorer sections of this community. You will receive my grace in all your efforts to serve the poor."*

Baba ended by saying, *"If ever you feel a sense of gratitude toward me, do give me some alms. Whatever you give to the poor, the neglected, the downtrodden brethren of yours with love, I shall receive it."* As the words ended and Baba's Divine body became still. His eyes remained wide open, but he was lost in the world beyond.

This episode not only reveals Baba's all-knowing Self, but also promotes the ideal of service to humanity as service to God. *"Whatever you offer with love to the poor and needy, I shall receive it."* Baba's words echo the profound words of Jesus:

"Come ye blessed of my Father, inherit the kingdom prepared for you from the foundation of the world: For I was hungry, and ye gave me meat; I was thirsty, and ye gave me drink; I was a stranger, and ye took me in; naked, and ye clothed me; I was sick and ye visited me; I was in prison and ye came unto Me.

> ".. Verily I say unto you, inasmuch as ye have done it unto one of the least of these my brethren, ye have done it unto me." (Matthew: 25.34)

Both Baba and Jesus were teaching the same lesson when they spoke these words. The one who gives should always be conscious that the true recipient of his gift is the Lord who resides in the hearts of all. Because Baba and Jesus are not separate from God they exist within all living things. Therefore, they taught that when love and devotion can be expressed through loving service to those who are in need, it is always God who is pleased. All actions are Divine actions when they are performed with a sincere wish to serve God. The essence of Karma Yoga is expressed in Baba's word, *"Serve, but serve consciously. Forget not the Doer as well as the Receiver of all actions."*

Baba warned the young man not to get drunk with power. This is what happens with most people in authority. It is no small wonder that the plight of the neglected and illiterate remains unchanged. Power corrupts. Absolute power corrupts absolutely. Baba only wanted to forewarn that power is a gift of the Divine and prudent person should utilize it for the betterment of his fellow human beings. Service to humanity is the path through which one can be released from the bondage of karma. It is the path of purification and leads to a state of egoless bliss.

MEDITATION

On Karma Yoga.

As you go through the day, cultivate mindfulness in the moment of doing. Consciously offer all you do to God. Make the smallest activity an oblation into the highest Divine purposes for creation. Work hard for God. Expend more energy and courage, go beyond what you would normally do or say, to make each effort the most beautiful gift you can lay on the altar. Find joy in the offering itself, releasing all outcomes to God.

Ask yourself at the end of the day: How much room do I make in my life and heart to serve God's work of uplifting the needy children of the divine? How could expand that dimension of my spiritual life? Ask for Baba's grace and guidance in showing you where you are called to give more.

CHAPTER 17

THE GOSPEL

It is only one who has reached the height of divine vision who can see the greatness and the glory of a living manifestation of the Divine. It is said that Bhagwan Sri Ramchandra, the Divine Incarnation, was only recognized by twelve Rishis.

Baba Lokenath often said, *"People think me a body. That's where they go wrong. I am not the body. How do I explain who I am? Even the thought of it makes me detached from my body. Therefore, the experience of that feeling cannot be expressed through the instrument of my mind."*

The most unusual feature of Baba's physical presence was his eyes, which were always wide open and as beautiful as lotus leaves. Baba never closed his eyes or even blinked in the twenty-six years that he lived at Baradi. He was an imposing figure at seven feet tall, with little flesh on his body. But through his yogic practices his skin looked supple and amazingly soft for one so bony.

His divine body was not subject to the usual physical manifestation such as hunger, thirst, sleep or disease. He had total control of the common natural tendencies of the human body. The harsh winters in the Himalayan could not deter him from his practices. He often told how heaps of snow would pile on his body as he did penance and then would melt away on its own during the summer.

Baba's divine body could be compared to the Imperishable Atman which is not affected by water, fire or any other natural element. When Vijay Krishna Goswami described Baba walking through the raging fire to save him, he said, "As the Mahatma walked through the fire with me on his shoulders, I had the feeling that the fire had totally lost its heat and our bodies were totally unaffected."

At the Baradi ashram no one ever saw Baba practicing yoga because he had already attained the ultimate. His primary purpose for the two decades at Baradi was to teach divinity as the first right of every individual. The truth is already here. It need only be accepted and realized. But Baba not only taught the truth. He was the living Truth.

Baba did not belong to any Sampradaya (any particular sect of the Hindu religion) or preach a particular path or method to reach God. He was available as the living Buddha. The seekers of diverse faiths, sects and traditions came to him, as did those who never believed in God or a Godman. He responded to the unique need of the moment to creatively foster each soul's natural evolution of consciousness. All the diverse paths which found their fulfillment in his divine Self flowed back out, through him, to the seekers of each path, leading them toward liberation.

The followers of different Hindu sects found in him the very embodiment of their path. He inspired and instructed those who came to him to find the Truth through the path of their own tradition. He was a Holy Confluence. Rivers came from diverse directions and merged into his oceanic expansion. Followers of Islam and Christianity also found in his divine presence the answers to any unresolved questions regarding their own path.

Transcending all sectarian religious barriers, Baba showed the way to the highest qualities of a humanity being true to itself. He showed how to reach from that foundation, through the life of the Spirit, into the divine. He showed the way home to the deep essence of our human existence.

To Muslim devotees Baba was a true Mussalman. He had not only learned and taught the Sacred Koran. He had lived it.

Jamini Kumar Mukhopadhaya, a very close disciple of Baba's, left us a rich treasure: the record of conversations he had with Baba Lokenath about different spiritual questions. These conversations give us a glimpse of the Mahapurusha and his unfathomable depth of wisdom. Baba's words offer the eternal principles of the universal religion of divine love and service. They transcend all limits of sectarianism, all narrow religious prejudice and dogma.

Here then, is an excerpt from Sri Jamini Kumar Mukhopadhaya's book entitled, "Dharmasar Sangraha."

Jamini: What is the meaning of the term 'taap'?
Baba: *It is the state of mind which happens as a consequence of the experience of sorrows, happiness, victory or defeat.*

Jamini: If the truth is that I can do whatever I please, then can I commit a sin such as theft or adultery?
Baba: *You cannot do that. Try and see, you cannot do that. As an individual advances on the path to the spirit, he or she cannot do such activities which are against the norms of the shastras or the society because that invariably brings a state of repentance on the individual. The phase that*

you have crossed, you usually do not return to, just as you cannot crawl on the floor like a child now that you have grown older.

Jamini: What is a sin?
Baba: *This is a personal issue. That which is right and should be the action for you may be wrong for another, and vice versa.*

Jamini: If I have a headache, I feel the pain of it. Then can a headache be understood as a sin?
Baba: *Yes.*

Jamini: I cannot understand how a headache could be considered sin.
Baba: *What is a head? Whose head? What is pain? Who feels pain? If you analyze all these questions you will realize that pain is the result of ignorance because in ignorance (Avidya) the pain is created, preserved and destroyed. Then you will understand that where there is Avidya or ignorance about the truth, there is the sin and the consequent unhappiness. In a state of Vidya, or realization, there is nothing like sin, pain or sorrow.*

Jamini: Baba, I do not see anything as free of miseries!
Baba: *You are right, He who performs all actions with this basic knowledge is a liberated one. There cannot be any action without a little bit of unhappiness attached to it; even God's creation is not beyond this natural law.*

Jamini: I cannot understand your saying that even God cannot create without a bit of sorrow attached to it.
Baba: *The root cause of all misery is ignorance. Even God does not perform the act of creation without the help of Ignorance, Avidya. Hence, all actions beget a bit of unhappiness.*

Jamini: Who is Guru?
Baba: *Obstacles! Wherever you are stuck you learn. You learn by lesson. The one whose instruction you follow is your Guru.*

Jamini: You should always remember your Guru. What is the significance of these words?
Baba: *Always remember the command of your Guru. The instruction or command is the Guru himself.*

Jamini: If the command of the Guru is the Guru himself, then can I disrespect the body of the Guru?
Baba: *No, people respect the container of the water of the Holy Ganges.*

Jamini: You should take refuge at the feet of the Master. What is the meaning if this?
Baba: *You should follow the path of your Master. That is the path which has led your Guru to the state of Shivatva (Godhood). You should follow it and act accordingly.*

Jamini: What is the meaning of giving an asana (seat) to the Guru?
Baba: *Offering a seat means that you must contemplate and concentrate on the instructions of your Master in you heart. Do not express his instructions to atheists and non-devotees.*
Jamini: Guruvat guru putrshu, What is the meaning of this?
Baba: *You must respect the worthy sons and grandsons of the Guru as you respect your Guru.*

Jamini: Who is the son of the Guru?
Baba: *The begotten child of the Guru or the one who has attained realization by following the instructions of the Guru.*

Jamini: If the son of the Guru is an illiterate fool, but still if I can show my devotion toward him, what is wrong?
Baba: *If is an ambiguous term. First, see whether you really can do it. If you do it only as an external show, then instead of doing good it will do harm to you.*

Jamini: When we have the Vedas, Tantra, Puranas, Guru Gita, Bhagavad Gita, Chandi (Chants to the Divine Mother), and other exalted spiritual texts, why should we need a Guru at all in life?
Baba: *The shastras (religious scriptures) can give you knowledge but not intuitive Wisdom. Nobody who does not have direct experience of the contents of these scriptures truly understands what these scriptures mean. If you carefully read all the shastras that you have just mentioned, you will see that each of these scriptures have explained in depth all about the goal and the path. But at the end of the reading, it would have said that you have to go to a realized Master to be enlightened to know the Reality. For example:*

> "Tad viddhi pranipatena pariprashnena sevaya upadekshyanti
> te jnanam jnaninas tattvadarshinah.
> (Bhagavad Gita 4/34)

(Learn by humble reverence, by inquiry and by service. The men of wisdom who have seen the truth will instruct thee in knowledge.)

Which means by serving the lotus feet of the Guru, by worshipping him and by continuously inquiring from him, that you will know the wisdom of the self. Tattvadarshi Guru that is the realized Master who would instruct you for your realization of Truth. That is the reason the Guru Gita proclaims:

> *'Na guror Adhikam, Na guror adhikam, Na guror adhikam.'*

There is none superior to the Guru. None superior to the Guru. None superior to the Guru. The Guru Gita repeats this thrice to emphasize its truth. Baba further quoted:

> *"Yajna dana tapo vrata japa tirthanusevanam gurutattvam avijnaya nishfalam natra samshayah."*

Without knowing what is 'Gurutattva' (what is Guru) if anyone takes to the path of yajna (the Vedic fire ritual), dana (charity), tapath (austerity), japa (the discipline of Mantra), or visits the Holy pilgrimages, all these virtuous efforts will, without doubt, be useless.

The shastras (scriptures) are the prime means to attain liberation. But one should practice these disciplines laid down in the scriptures only under the able guidance of the adept Guru.

Jamini: What is the duty of the Guru toward the disciple?
Baba: *He kindles the light of wisdom in the heart of the disciple. Who am I? What am I supposed to do in life? From where have I come? Where am I to go? What is the secret of this creation? He makes you seek solutions to these fundamental questions of life and guides you to realize them.*

Jamini: Why in the Guru Gita are there different types of mantras glorifying the qualities and attributes of the Guru?
Baba: *The Guru is infinite! His divine attributes and forms are unlimited. In the Guru Gita only a few of those divine attributes are mentioned. Depending upon the competence of the devotee, one would be able to understand or reach the true nature of the Guru and, accordingly, evolve into the subtle gradations of the realms of spiritual consciousness.*

Jamini: What is the cause of my bondage and ultimate freedom?

Baba: *There is one reason. One who binds you also frees you from bondage. She is Goddess, Mahamaya. She is the one who has created this entire cosmos. By worship, if you can please Her, She will bless and free you from bondage.*

You are bound by your tongue and sexual desire. When you are free of the attachments to these you will be free.

When you are hungry, eat. Eat as much as you need to appease your hunger. Do not eat more. When you are not hungry, or once you've had enough, don't eat out of greed or due to pressure from others. There is no need to go without food when you have hunger.

> *Meditate and worship your hunger. Don't worship greed or your tongue.*
> 'Yea Devi Sarva Bhuteshu Kshudha rupena samsthita.'
> (Chandi 5/28)

The Divine Mother manifests as hunger in all living beings. Therefore, eat while meditating, offering oblations to the fire of hunger in your stomach.

Jamini: How am I to know whether I am bound or free?
Baba: *The touchstone is the feeling of unhappiness. When you never feel unhappy either in pleasure or pain, insult or praise, cold or heat, when you remain in state of equanimity, then you can believe that you are Freed!*

Jamini: What is the cause of being unhappy in life?
Baba: *Desire is the root cause of all unhappiness. He who has no desire has no unhappiness in life.*

Jamini: When there is no action that can bring true bliss to human beings, and desire is the root of all miseries, why not give up 'all actions along with wife and children,' and accept 'Sannyas' (monkhood), and stay under the tree or in the mountains.
Baba: *Even if that is good, can you do that? For a while you may think that you are detached and dispassionate; but you would not be able to see the roots of the attachments and desires deep within your mind. You can't see them because you are blind to their reality. When you have deep-seated desires in you mind, even if you take sannyas and live under the trees you will not attain to sannyas. You will achieve only this — leaving your own wife, whom you accepted with your word to God, and accepting another woman to serve you!*

[Note: Baba makes it very clear that giving up externals and relationships is not renunciation. Renunciation is a state of mind drowned in the pure love of God. It is better to work with one's own mind in situations which help you to purge your tendencies and to recognize the need for fewer desires, more meditation, simple living, and high thinking. Living the householder's life can prepare one for a state of desirelessness and egolessness, which is the true state of Sannyas.]

Jamini: Is Sannyas a good state of mind?
Baba: *Yes, it is a good state of mind.*

Jamini: What is Sannyas?
Baba: *"The one who regards action and non-action as one and the same, he can be called a sannyasin. Those who renounce all actions and remain idle, they cannot be called sannyasin."*

[Note: Non-action is giving up action. In this state of mind the work happens through the yogi. He, however, remains a witness, just as we observe others working and do not become identified.]

Jamini: What are the three causes of sorrows in this world?
Baba: *This world is full of sorrows and miseries: 1) the shot of insulting word; 2) the shot of the loss of wealth; and 3) the shot of losing the most near and dear. These are the three cause of sorrow. One who can bear with patience these three shots can even conquer death.*

Jamini: Do you consider remaining active in the midst of these sorrows and unhappiness as the right attitude?
Baba: *Yes, I do consider it to be right, for action is better than inaction.*

[Note: Baba always stresses dynamism.]

Jamini: Is there any beneficial effect of these sorrows in life?
Baba: *Yes, there is a great beneficial effect on the life. Consider the lives of Sita and Prahlad. Do you understand the reason for the Divine Incarnation? The Almighty God descends to safeguard the interest of religion whenever the time is ripe. And He Himself practices religion and preaches it to the people.*

[Note: Baba as an Divine Incarnation practiced the disciplines, lived the truth and preached it.]

Jamini: In the case of Sita and Prahlad we see what awful tortures they had to tolerate to receive Divine Grace.
Baba: *Yes, that is true, but they never perished.*

Jamini: What lessons are we to take from the lives of Sita and Prahlad?
Baba: *In spite of intolerable miseries, when Sita stood in the midst of the fire, the fire could not touch her. The Lord Hari took Sita and Prahlad on His lap whenever they were forced to undergo physical torture.*

[Note: This reference is to Indian mythology: the Ramayana-Purana. Baba points to the truth that in the fire of agony the soul is processed and liberated. The devotee never perishes. Misery opens the gate to the realm of Divine Realization.]

Jamini: How is it that you are always free of any anxieties or any efforts?
Baba: *I am wise and you are ignorant. I know that I do not offer food to anybody. The one whose food is here, he gets it on his own accord. The one whose food is not here does not get it. I do not feel otherwise. You are afraid if you cannot offer food, you may have to face insults from the society. I have no such fear.*

[Note: Baba speaks here about the course of destiny. He who is destined to have food shall have. Baba is the witnessing self. He is unaffected by the words of the people!]

Jamini: If we contemplate on the higher qualities what will be the benefit?
Baba: *Just as darkness disappears with the rising of the sun, just as the thief runs away when the householder wakes up, in the same manner if you contemplate the higher qualities, the lower instincts will run away from you and your body will be transformed into a temple of the Divine. Later, when the power of Brahman awakens in you, you will become Brahman.*

Jamini: Is there any method by which the body and mind can be purified?
Baba: *Yes, there is. Sattwic food purifies the body, and the renunciation of desires purifies the mind. When your body and mind are purified then you will realize Hari. Then you will know what Hari is to you.*

[Note: Hari refers to Lord Vishnu the sustainer of this Universe. Pure vegetable foods are always good for body and mind. It always keeps the mind calm. In spiritual life pure vegetarian and fresh foods are considered Sattwic. That which gives us stable mind.]

Jamini: The power of Brahman will manifest itself in my heart. What is the meaning of this?
Baba: *Why, have you not seen the image of the Mother Kali worshipped on the Mahastami day?*

Jamini: Yes, I have seen it, but what am I to understand from that?
Baba: *That Kali is the Brahman-Shakti, the potential energy of Brahman. She is standing on the dead body.*

Jamini: Who is the dead body?
Baba: *You all know him as Shiva.*

Jamini: Why do you call the dead body Shiva?
Baba: *The reason is that Shiva is Shav or dead!*

Jamini: Shiva is also known as Mritunjay, the conqueror of death, then why do you call Shiva Shav or dead?
Baba: *The reason for which He is the Immortal One is the reason to call Him shav or dead.*

Jamini: I cannot understand. What is that reason?
Baba: *By renouncing all desires, when one reaches a state of desirelessness, immortality is attained. The destruction or annihilation of the pot (body) is death. But the one who does not identify with the body does not die. How can there be the phenomenon of death to one who has no ego? In this state, all*

actions of day-today life are performed without the sense of doing. In the absence of desire the Jiva (Individual) moves about in this world like the living dead. The moment an individual reaches a state of desirelessness, 'Jivatava,' that is, worldly identification ceases and the state of 'Shivatva,' Godhood, is attained. 'Jivabhav,' the tendencies of worldliness are transformed and merge into the Existential Being of Brahman. In that state the Potential Divine Energy, Brahmashakti, takes possession of the living dead. And through the body of the living dead, She performs Her actions of Creation, Preservation and Annihilation. Thus endowed with Divine qualities, the Jiva or individual soul comes to be known as Shiva, God in human form.

Jamini: If I reach a state of desirelessness, am I to see the form of the four-armed mother Kali within my heart?
Baba: *'Sadhakaanam hitarthya brahmano rupakalpanam.' I hope you know the meaning of this.*

Jamini: Yes, I know, but please explain further.
Baba: *The Formless Absolute Reality (Brahman) assumes form in order to bless the seeker with the divine vision of the chosen deity.*

[Note: Baba says that the Formless assumes form in *order to please the devotee who longs to see God in a particular form.]*

Jamini: How many categories of Spiritual seekers are there?
Baba: *Four types : 1) Jnani 2) Bhakta 3) Karmi 4) Yogi*
Those who are Jnanis say Brahman (pure consciousness) is Jnanaswarupa, meaning Infinite wisdom, Omniscient. Those who are Bhaktas (devotees) say that God is with form (as you see in the Gods of Hindu). *Those who are Yyogis say Karma is Brahman (*action is inseparable from God). *Yogis say that Atman is Brahman* (the individual self is one with the Cosmic Self).

Jamini: Is there any difference in the technique and method among these four types of spiritual disciplines?
Baba: *Yes, the spiritual discipline of a Jnani is Satsanga (the company of the holy Ones or study of scriptures), Dana (giving), Vichara (discrimination between the eternal and the transient) and Santosh (contentment). The discipline of Yoga is to unite the Jivatman (individual soul) with the Pramatman (the Supreme Godhead) or to awaken the Kundalini and allow it to merge with the Pranam Shiva, the Supreme Godhead or to unite Radha with Krishna. The discipline of Bhakti is to worship the Divine and serve Him as one would do to one's own self. The discipline of Karma is Dana (giving), Yajna (sacrificial fire), the performance of all worldly activities in a spirit of dispassion and detachment. Though I have spoken about the four types of disciplines of yoga, all spiritual seekers —regardless of the path followed— have to perform all actions with awareness and discrimination, thereby reaching the state of desirelessness, to become liberated.*

Jamini: What is the benefit of Satsanga, the company of the Holy Ones?
Baba: *The glory of the company of Holy Ones is beyond human expression.*

Jamini: What is the benefit of Dana or gifting?
Baba: *It helps you enrich your feeling for others and attain renunciation.*

Jamini: What is the benefit of Vichara?
Baba: *It helps you realize the difference between the Atman and the Anatman. When your consciousness of discrimination between the eternal and the transient awakens, you become truly detached. Then the Jiva becomes Shiva. That is, man becomes God.*

Jamini: What is the way to inculcate the sense of contentment?

Baba: *To try constantly to keep the mind in a state of happiness by being God-conscious under all circumstances. While attending to all one's mundane day-to-day activities.*

Jamini: If one is blessed with Divine vision, why does he not attain liberation?
Baba: *It is only through suffering that the 'Prarabdha karma' ends.*

Jamini: What is Prarabdha karma?
Baba: *The Wise Ones have compared Prarabdha karma with arrows. Just as the archer does not have any control over the arrow which has left the bow, the arrow, depending upon its speed, falls at a distance. So also is the Prarabdha karma of the Jivas (individual souls)*

Jamini: I did not understand you clearly.
Baba: *Have you not read in your childhood days, 'Lalate Likhitam yattu sasthi jagar vasare. Na Hari Shankaro Brahma cha anyatha kartum iti?' The meaning of 'sasthi' is the sum total of six, not loosely or separately, but by being one. Jagar Vasare is an awakened state. The meaning of the sloka is: Before the creation when the Absolute Brahman was One, and He willed 'Ekameva bahushyam' ('I Am One, but let me be many'), the whole creation came onto existence. At that time, whatever is written on the forehead of one, that is whatever activity is prescribed for one by the will of the Lord, even Brahma, Vishnu and Maheshwara are bound by that wish. This wish is the Prarabdha.*

Jamini: Why during devotional chants and Japa (repetition of Divine Name) or meditation do I feel inner bliss?
Baba: *Because at that time you are not thinking about or engaged in the work of your tongue or sex.*

According to Baba, depending upon the nature of the seeker, all kinds of fire ritual, worship, and meditation are imperative in the life of human beings. He gave mantra to some and allowed others to perform all the Hindu rituals of worship. He advised that the worship of Shiva, Krishna, and Kali are highly beneficial to the soul in the search of the Divine.

Baba once told Jamini, *"Your mother tells you to eat a little more. She is encouraging you in the enjoyment of more food. Your father says don't eat more; if you eat more you will fall sick. He is pointing you toward the path of sacrifice. And I am telling you, 'Jamini, you have neither enjoyment, nor renunciation. You are neither bhogi (pleasure seeker) nor tyagi (renounced one). You are unchangeable, immutable ancient Purusha (Self). You are eternally blissful; you have never the trace of sin in you."*

Jamini ends this diary with the words, "Blessed I am that I could sit at the feet of such a Satguru. This must be because of the good deeds of many previous births and blessings of the ancestors."

Baba's wisdom flowed unceasingly to all who would listen. On rare occasions he would share his feelings. Once, talking to the devotees, Baba Lokenath said, "After decades of traveling throughout the length and breadth of the world, when I landed at Baradi, I felt a deep urge to give, to give all that I had brought along with me. But I could hardly find anybody who was prepared to receive that which I came to 'distribute.'

Baba said, "Once I had a doubt in my mind whether I had become Brahman. So, to find out, I cured ninety-four nearly dying patients just by means of my word. As a result the entire ashram premises turned into a big hospital. But the people mistook me for a doctor of physical ailments, when I came to cure the disease of worldly life."

In the Bhagavad Gita, Bhagwan Sri Krishna says :

> "O Arjuna! He is a perfect yogi who considers all beings as dear as his own Self and shares in the happiness and sorrows of others as very much his own." (6.32 Bhagavad Gita)

The equal vision of Baba Lokenath was all encompassing. From the smallest living creatures, to the most highly spiritually advanced yogis from the Himalayas and Tibet to demi-gods and goddesses, he showered his boundless compassion and grace on all alike. Baba Lokenath said, *"I have traveled in the hills and mountains for more than a century. Heaps of snow piled over my body and melted on its own, but I could not meet your God anywhere. I have seen only Myself. I am bound by my own karma. The materialistic world is bound by the tongue and the sex organ. He who can restrain these two is fit to attain Siddhi."*

This is the highest state as described in the Bhagavad Gita. The yogi sees within himself the all-pervasive Brahman, and in the all-pervasive Brahman, he sees himself. This is total Unified Being.

As a result of this realization, the yogi completely identifies himself with objective manifestations. The subjective and objective merge into each other in a divine harmony. All the walls of difference disappear and sama darshana, equal vision, rules the heart of the yogi. Compassion becomes as natural and spontaneous as breathing.

Love manifests through the yogi as fragrance to flowers. Love is not an action but a state of being. To the Realized One love happens, contrasted with the love of unrealized worldly beings where love is always mixed with hate. The man with ego can never love. It is a mere ego manifestation. That is the reason we find that in worldly relationships the slightest provocation or unfavorable circumstance will quickly reduce love to dislike or even to hatred.

The love that manifests in a yogi never turns into hate. In him love is unconditional. This is true love in the purest sense of the term. And true love is possible only where the ego has been transformed into divinity. Therefore, love is a divine manifestation. Love is God. Love is Divinity.

Once Baba was asked what motivated him to come down from the heavenly abode of the Himalayas. He replied, *"When I reached the state of identifying myself with all living manifestations, I could not but feel the pain and suffering of all as if they were happening to me. I could see the Brahman, the one Existential Truth, living in all. Hence, the question of heaven and hell was no longer anywhere to be seen. For all was He."*

The Enlightened One is free from pride and ignorance and is never attached to his action or its fruit. He is ever illumined in the conscious awareness of the Divine, unaffected by the opposites of pleasure and pain, by love and hatred of the mundane plane. He moves about in the world as the living God, in a state of absolute detachment and desirelessness.

From dawn to dusk Baba Lokenath kept busy performing a multitude of activities in the ashram. People came from near and far to receive his guidance and divine grace. But even a little close observation on the part of the devotees would reveal the truth that Baba remained ever detached and lost in his Transcendental Self. How can the one who is established in his own Self be disturbed by any external influence of the objective world? Those who had come in close contact with this living Buddha had seen in him the simplest expression of this excellent sloka of the Gita:

> "Niramana-moha-jita-sanga-dosa adhyatma-nitya
> vinivrtta-kamah"
> Dvandvair-vimuktah sukha-dukha-samjnair -gacchanty-
> amuydhah padam-avayam tat"
> (15.5 Bhagavad Gita)

Lord Krishna says in the Gita that the yogi, who, after attaining self-realization, compassionately works for the good and benefit of the people, for their spiritual and material emancipation, is the dearest of all. He is the most perfect of yogis.

It is only through deep, Divine intoxication and profound compassion that Baba boldly spoke to his children of immortality, *"I have traveled in the hills and mountains, and have earned enough treasures; you enjoy them sitting at home."* This declaration underlines, once again, the depth of Baba's unconditional love. He stood as a living example of his own interpretation of the Bhagavad Gita, that the Gita is not merely a book to be read, but a song, a melody, a symphony which is sung by the Supreme Lord sitting in your heart. Once you are drunk with its melody, you will be transformed from an ordinary mortal into a divine being.

Baba had once told his devotees, *"Even if a yogi two hundred years of age comes to me, if he is not in my state, I shall consider him as a child.*

I allow you to reach me, hence, you can reach me, otherwise your might is too little for it."

These words are the expressions of Baba's Total Divinity, for it is the Divine which is beyond the reach of mind and intellect.

Baba said, *"I am Eternal, I shall never perish, hence, there is no question of the last ceremonial rites for this body. People take me to be a man. That is where they make the greatest blunder. I can do whatever I like. You have no trust, however, so your desires remain unfulfilled. Let Shraddha (trust in the words of the Guru and Shastra) be your shelter. Let Shraddha be your friend and the path to Realization.*

MEDITATION

Hold the following quote in your heart as you go into meditation: "In spite of intolerable miseries, when Sita stood in the midst of the fire, the fire could not touch her. In the fire of agony, the soul is processed and liberated."

Recall any unhealed wounds of your life, past or present, and the pain they cause you. Vividly imagine that pain as a purifying fire---one which burns away all that keeps you from the Divine and from where God is leading you. Then surrender yourself and the pain into the white heat of those flames. Allow all that you have known yourself to be burned away, to be reduced to purified molten light which is ready to be recast in the hands and heart of the Divine. Trust that even your pain is God's love for you, showing you where you need to go, guiding you home to the Divine. (Whenever you are in pain, difficulty, or crisis, repeat this meditation.)

CHAPTER 18

FAREWELL: "I AM WITH YOU"

DEATH IS A phenomenon of the body. That which is born is destined to decay and die in time, but the *Atman* is birthless and deathless. It is Eternal.

The One who is birthless assumes the human body only to establish the Truth of the Spirit, to protect and nourish the good. The One does not punish, but reforms those caught in darkness by inspiring them to take the path of light. Taking a human body, The One is unlike others who are grossly body-identified and remains ever in a state of yoga with Existence-Consciousness-Bliss Infinite. The *Jivanmukta* (who is in the body yet eternally free) is God in human form.

Baba Lokenath was the *Jivanmukta,* whose coming uplifts human beings all over the world to become one with God. Though Baba distributed wealth, prosperity and healing to many, his abundant spiritual gifts and blessings are the real boon of his time on earth. And they are extended to all.

We have seen the Divine Play of his life. He worked with devotees' minds to check their tendencies towards evil and vice. He inspired confidence and faith in the Self and helped them move toward the light of the spirit. In his lifespan of 160 years, he embodied the attributes and qualities of God.

As Gwalini Ma puts it in her simple words, "Nothing could be hidden from Baba. He knew all my thoughts with absolute clarity." Thousands who visited Baradi shared that experience. Baba had incredible command and access to people's minds, which he used to inspire faith and show the way to self-correction.

Baba Lokenath would often say, *"People commit the gravest mistake by thinking of me as a person, as a body."* Even Arjuna could not understand the truth that Sri Krishna, who was his friend and charioteer, was God Himself. It was only when Lord Krishna granted him Divine Vision that he had the eyes to see the Universal Form of the All-Pervading Brahman in Lord Krishna.

"I am Eternal, Imperishable, ever Existent." Baba spoke thus about the supreme state of his total identification with the *Paramatman.* His divinized body had few qualities of material phenomenon.

He once told a close devotee that he was living beyond the time of his destined life. *"At this state, if I allow sleep to happen, this body will fall* (die)." No one had ever seen him sleeping or close his eyes. At night he would lean back on the wooden plank you see in his picture for a few moments, and take rest in an awakened state.

Enlightened Ones do not die. The Buddha gives up the body at will. Prabhupada Vijay Krishna Goswami had said again and again that Baba is totally free. He could leave his body at any moment, whenever he wished, or he could retain it for time eternal. The

Liberated Ones, however, always follow natural laws, even though they are beyond them.

The naked sannyasin who walked into the village of Baradi along with Dengu Karmakar around the year 1864 spent twenty-six long years there, gradually revealing his Divinity. Above all else, he flooded the land with his boundless compassion and love. Like the rains, they were showered impartially. Everyone had their share, depending on their spiritual effort and trust in the Divine Presence of Baba.

During those years Baba had demonstrated the living manifestation of the Divine Play, that of God in human form, the *"Nara-lila,"* as Sri Ramakrishna called it.

Baba found it difficult to remain in his physical cage that last year. He would often forget the existence of his body. Then, a few months before his *mahasamadhi*, one of Baba's devotees surrendered to Baba's will the life of his only son. The young boy had a severe case of tuberculosis and was dying. Baba saw the boy and pronounced that his inevitable death would occur within a short time. The father of the boy, shocked to hear this from Baba, said, "Baba, no one returns from your ashram unfulfilled. Nothing is impossible for you. I know that if you show mercy the boy will live." The man was sobbing. Baba's heart melted. He said, *"Very well, I have taken the disease in my body. Now you can go."* The boy was cured of the disease. Within four to five months, however, the boy died of other causes.

Soon after curing the boy, Baba began to show symptoms of the terrible illness. Baba had decided to leave his body. Although he suffered the virulent coughing attacks with absolute detachment, his body began deteriorating.

One of Baba's devotees became quite concerned, though he had often seen Baba absorb the diseases of devotees and suffer them in his body. Until then Baba had only suffered for very short periods. The dreadful symptoms of disease would just manifest in his *Yoga-siddha* body like a passing cloud. Baba always had remained as unaffected as the sky. However, this time his physical condition continued to deteriorate from day to day.

It became clear that Baba had decided to leave his one hundred sixty year old temple to enter into the hearts of his millions and millions of dear children all over the world.

Just eight days before his *mahasamadhi* Baba asked his devotees, *"Can you tell me what is the right way to perform the last rites for a dead body?"* A few answered that the best way was to burn the body. Others favored burying the body in a graveyard. The last group was in favor of committing the body to the Ganges. Baba added that there was yet another method, leaving the body in an isolated place where it could be eaten by vultures and other animals.

He then further questioned the group. *"What do you think is the quickest method of destroying a dead body?"* Most of the devotees favored burning the dead body on a funeral pyre. Baba declared, *"When my body falls, burn it to ashes."*

Observing the failing condition of his health, Baba decided to give up his body promptly. The date and time for leaving the body was a matter of his own choosing. He declared to his devotees that on the 19th day of Jaistha, (June 2nd), 1890, he would leave his mortal body and enter *mahasamadhi.*

Nothing could have been more shocking and heartbreaking to the children of Baba. Their lives had been spontaneously transformed the moment they had taken shelter in his Divinity. Baba's presence during the most critical times of their lives had inspired such confidence and trust in them that they had always enjoyed a state of fearlessness. Most devotees had such total trust in his Divine powers that they would often express the feeling that even *Yama,* the god of death, had to bow before his will. It was only when Baba willed it that a devotee could die.

In his state of enlightened wisdom, Baba considered his body only a worldly manifestation composed of the five basic elements. They would decompose and mix with the elements of Mother Nature. He was the Presence, unchanging and endless.

But how can ignorant human beings conceive of this abstraction that is so beyond their personal experience? They know the body, not the *Atman.* Their attachment was more to the body than to the Eternal *Paramatman,* which was Baba's true being. Baba's announcement left them crying bitterly and feeling utterly helpless. They repeatedly pleaded with Baba to have pity, "How can you leave us so soon? How can you be so merciless as to leave us orphaned? If you were going to leave us so soon, why did you bring us to your Holy Presence? Why have you loved us so much?"

Men and women, both young and old, began arriving at the ashram. Persistently, they tried to persuade Baba to reconsider. They were convinced that his departure was only a matter of his preference, so it could be postponed to a distant future date. Baba responded to the pleading and prayers with compassion and love, *"After this body falls, do not think that everything will come to an end. After I leave this gross body, I will live in the hearts of all living beings in my subtle form. Whoever seeks my refuge will always receive my grace."*

He also said, *"If I leave the body during the day, in the period of Uttarayana, and if the sun is shining very brightly in a clear sky on that day, then you can be sure that I have penetrated the solar system (Surya Mandal) and have transcended beyond. Whether I reincarnate or not is up to my will."*

This refers to the eighth chapter of the *Bhagavad Gita* and to the *Chandogya Upanishad.* (4.15.5)

The Knower of Supreme Brahman attains the Ultimate state of Absolute Brahman if he leaves his mortal body at the time of *Agni* and *Jyotis* (presiding deity of bright fortnight) and of Uttarayana (presiding deity of the six months of the Sun's passing to the north of the equator).

The coincidence of these principles of *Agni, Jyotis* and *Uttarayana* are considered most auspicious. We find Baba selecting the 19th day of *Jaistha* (June 2) with this in mind. His saying 'if' the sun shines bright was only to honor the injunctions of the *shastras,* for he was well aware that the Sun God always serves the intentions of the *Brahmarishi.*

The sky was ominous and the mood at the ashram was somber as the day of Baba's departure approached. For the devotees, the ruthless reality of death seemed to be nature's most cruel law.

On the 18th of Jaistha (June 1) the sky remained cloudy. A few showers brought some relief from the heat. The devotees of Baba held on to the hope that, if the sky remained gloomy, the next day Baba might change his mind. But the wish of the Enlightened One is the Wish of God. The Sun God prepared his chariot to take the Blessed One to the abode of Brahman. On the morning of the 19th of Jaistha, the sky was clear and the sun was radiant.

Disciples and devotees had come from every direction. They gathered in the ashram for their last darshan with Baba in his physical presence.

Early in the morning of June 2, 1890, Ramkumar Chakraborty came to the ashram. He talked with Baba privately for some time. Then Baba instructed him to perform the last ceremonial rites after the *mahasamadhi.*

About ten o'clock in the morning, Baba called his devotees. He wanted them to have their food. No one was in the mood, but it was the last instruction of the Master. Baba supervised the serving of the food. When the last person in the ashram had received the blessed food, Baba went inside his room to sit on his *asana* in his usual *gomukhasana* posture.

The devotees sat near Baba, expecting that out of mercy for his children, he would change his mind. Silence prevailed in the room. With his non-blinking lotus eyes, Baba looked at all the devotees and disciples and said in the most compassionate voice:

> *"My children! Why are you all so worried? Do you think I am going to die? Only this old worn-out body will fall. I am ever-present. I am deathless.*

"If, with a little touch of love and devotion, you call me, you will instantly feel how close I am to you. As I heard your words in the body, so shall I hear when this body is no more. Just as you are receiving my grace now, you shall always receive my protection and grace in the future. This is my promise.

"Where can I go? In all existence, I am eternally present.

"Whoever will seek my eternal Presence and my grace with right trust and surrender, will experience me.

With steadfast devotion, hold on to the Truth. Surrender yourself with sincerity to the Divine and move along the path shown by Satguru.

"The yoga of Self-Realization is the path to freedom. Devotion and love is the essence. Mantras are the props. With devotion and love, move ahead fearlessly. Who is there to obstruct your way? You are my children.

"No one can rule over my children. I have never preached. This is the place of command.
You are never alone. I am always with you. Never forget this truth. I am eternally present in you. I shall remain with you for posterity.

"I am Eternal. I am Deathless."

For the last time, the crowd of assembled devotees heard the words of love and compassion from the Living God. Like the nectar of the Vedas, his immortal words had come down, flowing like the holy water of the Ganges. From the lofty heights of the Himalayas to the plains, they came to soothe the burning hearts of those who suffered and those who ached to be reborn to a higher purpose.

The thunderous voice proclaimed the Vedic revelation, *"Fear not, I am with you."* He wants his children to move fearlessly in daily life, with utmost self-confidence and trust in Him. Brahmarishi Baba Lokenath blessed his beloved devotees with his non-blinking eyes. In the next moment, he proceeded through the crown of his head, through the solar rays, to the ultimate union of *mahasamadhi*. He returned to the Pure Field of Eternal Existence, the realm from which he sojourned here for the sake of all who suffer, to bring them solace and peace, and to show them the path of life and light and the blessedness of their birthright beyond suffering.

Baba's *mahasamadhi* too was quite unique! He was merged with the Divine through the *mahasamadhi*, but his body remained in its yogic posture, with his non-blinking eyes wide open. The devotees were uncertain, since they had often seen Baba in that seemingly lifeless state of *samadhi*. But that was for a short while. This time Baba did not show any sign of life for a long time.

Penetrating the sun, the source of light and life for this world, Baba reached beyond. He became the Eternal Sun of the spiritual sky, the Source of Enlightenment diffusing Light and Love throughout the world, working silently in the hearts of all for their spiritual transformation.

At about eleven forty-five in the morning, the devotees touched Baba's body and found that he had left it for good. The whole atmosphere was charged with thundering voices shouting, "Jai Baba Lokenath! Glory to Baba Lokenath!" Devotees, young and old, were overcome with emotion. They burst into tears. They were still unable to comprehend the finality of Baba's departure. While they knew in their hearts that Baba would always be with them, they were deeply pained to face the reality that their beloved Baba Lokenath would no longer be present in his Divinized body to hear their problems and reassure them with his inspiring and fearless counsel.

The old mother of the ashram Gwalini Ma could not restrain herself. By Baba's grace, she had risen to a high state of detachment. Now her wisdom melted in profuse tears. She held his body with possessive tenderness, questioning why such a loving child could leave this world without taking his old mother along. She begged and begged for her Divine Child and Guru to come back, but this samadhi was final.

The devotees carried the body of Baba and placed it under the bael tree. Word spread like wildfire far and wide. Thousands of villagers of all faiths came running to the ashram. They could not believe that Baba could die. This was an emptiness that could never be filled.

From the poorest of the poor to the richest of the rich, people came with Ghee (clarified butter) and sandalwood to prepare the last bed of the funeral pyre. They showered thousands of flowers and garlands over the Divine body. Even the most reclusive women, who never came out in public, forgot their taboos and fell into uncontrollable weeping at Baba's feet for a last touch of their beloved.

The funeral pyre was lit by Ramkumar. Rising flames consumed the perishable body. The five elements of earth, water, fire, air, and ether were returned to their elemental form. The devotees filled the air with chants of the Divine name of God Incarnate, Baba Lokenath.

Thus ended this Divine Play of God in human form in this mortal world. His Play continues in the Eternal Realm. It has no beginning and no end. The synthesis of yoga, which he taught the world for over two decades at Baradi, sowed the seeds of Divinity in his children. He was preparing them for the world of tomorrow, when they will usher in an era of Truth and Blessedness.

After Baba Lokenath left his mortal body, his teachings and living ideals spread far and wide, touching all of Asia. It was a gradual development. This is true of all the Enlightened Ones. During their life, only a very few are privileged to come into their physical presence. Fewer still grasp the Divinity they embody. Once they leave their physical body, their spiritual vibrations spread and silently work wonders in the hearts of devotees. They come to be worshipped as a Living Incarnation of God by millions and millions of people as time passes.

Today Baba is no longer in his physical body. Millions of devotees feel his Presence and feel in their hearts that Baba is always with them in times of distress and also in happiness.

Lokenath is eternal. His words of assurance are also eternal. His Promise, *"Whenever you are in danger, whether in war, forest, ocean or jungle, remember Me. I shall save you,"* can be tested and trusted. His assurance, *"I have traveled in the hills and mountains extensively and have earned enough spiritual treasure, you will sit at home and enjoy the fruits of my austerities"* calls us to join him in the heights of spiritual attainment.

Baba Lokenath both lived and practiced the principles which Lord Krishna preached in the *Bhagavad Gita*. 'The Living Gita' embodied the glorious heritage of India, the land of spirituality, by demonstrating that real peace and bliss come only through the practice of restraint and spiritual awareness. Bliss does not exist in the materialistic world. It exists within the heart. It can be attained through conscious effort, through the will to rise above the bondage of attached action. Baba lived Truth. He taught the synthesis of *Jnana, Bhakti, Karma* and *Astanga Yoga* as the ultimate alchemy.

Today, the ashram of Baradi remains a holy pilgrimage site for millions of Hindus, Muslims and Christians, as well as for devotees of other religions. The Gita, the Koran and the Bible are all manifested in the Divine life of Baba Lokenath.

Lokenath is the Sun. Where Lokenath dwells, the darkness of ignorance, fear and unhappiness is dispelled. Seek his grace with trust and love. He will be with you. He is the Perennial River of Spiritual Grace, ever- flowing. You need only take his *Madhunam* (his Transcendental Sweet Name) and drink the nectar of his love to be lifted from unhappiness and anguish into spiritual awakening, eternal peace, and bliss.

Sitting in the hearts of his devotees, the Indwelling Light sparks with the words of eternal assurance. 'The Living Shiva' keeps dancing and singing:

"Oh! My children! When are you going to believe that I alone am the Doer? Trust and rely upon me. Give up your unreal sense of doership. Perform your duties with sincerity and dedication. Leave everything to me. You will surely attain peace.

"Whoever will seek my presence and grace at times of distress and danger will feel my healing grace instantly.

"I have left the body, but to protect my devotees from any danger I am always with them. You do not recognize me because you don't have the eyes to see.

"The more you will have faith and trust in me the more you will have the fulfillments of your wishes in life. Nobody leaves me empty handed. Those who surrender to me will attain to their coveted goals. Don't be engrossed with the world's mundane demands and forget the Self. Realize the Truth. My grace will quickly help you to achieve your spiritual quest.

"Know with certainty that I carry the burden of my devotees on my own shoulders. All your responsibilities are mine. Just give me your simple heart and mind.

"I am a beggar for your love. My mercy spreads all over the world. Ask for it with trust and love. Pick it up.

"He who gives their whole heart and mind to me alone, I become theirs. I am eternally indebted to them.

In you, I live as the timeless Truth. I am ever awake. I feel happy when you are happy, unhappy when you feel unhappy.

" I am the imperishable Self. I am. I am. I am."

Sarve bhavantu sukhinah
Sarve santu niramayah

Sarve bhadrani pasyantu
Ma kaschit dukkha bhag bhavet.
Om Shanti Om Shanti Om Shanti

May all be happy, may all enjoy sound physical and mental health, may all see good in others and in everything, may none in this world suffer from miseries and unhappiness. May Peace be everywhere!

MEDITATION

Read and reread the promises and assurances of Baba above. Let their truth and light and energy pour into your heart. Let them flood your being. Absorb the power and love which the Divine sends out to you through them. In prayer and meditation, direct the magnitude of that love toward all that holds you back in life, sweeping it away. Let Baba, and the sweet roaring force of the Divine Love in these promises, carry you, today and everyday, to the heights of light for which you are meant.

GLOSSARY

Acharya: Spiritual preceptor, teacher.

Adharma: Absence of duty, law, righteousness, virtue.

Advaita: Non-duality.

Adiguru: The original Guru; Guru of Gurus.

Anatman: The non-self; denotes everything that is experienced as being different from the Transcendental Self.

Antaryamin Guru: Spiritual preceptor who is considered to be omniscient.

Arjuna: The warrior hero of the Bhagavad Gita. One of the Pandava brothers.

Asana: Yoga position or posture of the body in meditation or exercise.

Ashram: Spiritual community, Spiritual school. A retreat Center.

Astanga yoga: Patanjali's eightfold path of Yogic discipline of Transcendence.

Atman: The Self or Soul; denotes also the Supreme Soul, with which, according to non-dualistic Vedanta philosophy, the individual soul is identical in essence, the immanent aspect of the Godhead.

Avatar: An incarnation of God. The descent of the Divine in the divinized body of the enlightened. The God in human form. Born for the redemption of suffering souls.

Atmarama: Established in the Self; Self content; Established in the Self the yogi witnesses the divine play.

Badrikashram: A holy pilgrimage site dedicated to Lord Vishnu situated in the Himalayas.

Bael: A tree whose fruit's leaves are sacred to Shiva.

Bhagavad Gita: Lit., The "Song of God". The eighteen chapters of this work are part of the Indian Epic, the Mahabharata.

Bhakti: Love relationship with Personal God; Devotion to God, Love of God; It is one of the main spiritual disciplines of Hinduism. The devotee loves God with heart and soul, expecting no worldly return from Him.

Bharat: A brother of Sri Rama. The land of Bharat refers to India.

Brahma: The creator God; the First Person of the Hindu Trinity, of which the other two members are Vishnu and Shiva.

Brahma Jnana: God Realization.

Brahmacharin: The seeker who has taken the vow of celibacy and total dedication to God.

Brahmacharya: Lit., "Brahmic conduct" Essentially stands for the ideal of chastity. The aspirant is asked to emulate the genderless condition of Brahman so as to preserve and and cultivate the great power inherent in the semen.

Brahman: The Absolute; the Ultimate Reality, the All Pervading Existence. The Supreme Reality of Vedanta Philosophy.

Brahmin: A member of the priestly caste, the highest caste in Hindu society.

Brahma Loka: The region of Brahman which corresponds the highest heaven of dualistic regions where spiritually evolved souls go after death.

Brahmo-Samaj: A socio-religious reform movement in India founded by Raja Rammohan Roy, 1774-1833.

Bal bhog: Morning food which Baba used to take between 9 a.m. and 9:30 a.m.

Buddha: "The enlightened One": The word refers specifically to Gautama Buddha, 560-480 BC. Born as Prince Siddhartha, he renounced the world to become one of the great spiritual teachers of all time, and the founder of Buddhism.

Chakra: Wheel; plexus; center: the seven psychological centers in the subtle body located along the spinal cord, at the crown, between eyebrows, throat, heart, navel, abdomen, and the base of the spine.

Chaitanya Mahaprabhu: Prophet born in 1485 A.D. Who lived in Bengal, who emphasized the path of divine love for the realization of God.

Darshan: Paying respects to a holy place or person by a ceremonial visit. The blessing or purification felt in the presence of holiness.

Devotee: The word is used in this book to denote one devoted to God, generally a follower of the path of love. A devotee of Baba Lokenath is one who is devoted to him and follows his teachings.

Dharana: Concentration.

Dharma: Duty, law, righteousness, virtue; in Hinduism it denotes the law of inner growth determined by man's actions in his past lives, which influence his present way of live.

Dhruba: A boy devotee of Vishnu. Also, known as the Polar Star.

Dhyana: Deep meditative state.

Draupadi: Wife of the Pandava princes in the Mahabharata daughter of King Drupad.

Gayatri Mantra: The most sacred and famous mantra of Hinduism which has been recited since ancient Vedic times.

Gomukhasana: Yoga posture. Baba's photograph shows him sitting in this posture.

Golden Age: Refers to that age when the majority of the people all over the world follow the path of truth and righteousness, love and sacrifice.

Gods and goddesses: Gods and goddesses are the different forms of One Absolute Self executing this divine play of creation, preservation and annihilation of myriads of life forms.

Guna, Gunas: The three qualities characterizing the primordial substance, the principal building blocks of nature which bind the embodying self to a particular body. The qualities are Sattva-purity, harmony; Rajas-emotion, action; Tamas-inertia, darkness.

Guru: The enlightened Master; spiritual preceptor, teacher.

Gurubhakti: Devotion to the Master.

Hari: God; One of the many names of Vishnu or Krishna.

Integral Yoga: The path of synthesis of Jnana yoga, Karma yoga, Bhakti yoga and Patanjali's Astanga yoga.

Jagadguru: World Teacher.

Japa: The practice of repeating the Holy Name of God; usually one's own mantra.

Jatishmara: A person who can recall past lives from birth.

Jivanmukta: One who has attained Liberation while living in the body.

Jnana: Knowledge; wisdom; comprehension.

Kali: A name of the Divine Mother. Kali symbolizes the dynamic aspect of Spirit, the primal energy.

Kama: Fulfillment of desire, one of the four goals of human pursuit.

Kali Yuga: The iron age. The age of divisive forces. Violence, untruths, false vanity of the self, rule this age. The only good aspect of this Kali is that those who are devoted to God and will chant the name of God will be freed from its clutch of misery.

Karma: Action in general; the chain of cause and effect operating in the moral world.

Kamakshya: The ancient Temple dedicated to the Divine Mother. The Greatest seat of Shakti, the Divine Energy, situated on the top of a Hill at the city of Guwahati, the capital of Assam State, in northeast India.

Khichri: A boiled food of a mixture of rice and lintels.

Koran: The Holy Book of Islam.

Krishna: One of the most widely worshipped Incarnations in Hinduism.

Kurukshetra: The battlefield on which Krishna instructed Arjuna in the Bhagavad Gita.

Lokenath: Lit., the Master of all the worlds-physical and metaphysical.

Kalpataru: The Wish-Fulfilling Tree. According to the Hindu mythology, whatever is wished sitting under the Kalpataru comes true instantly.

Lakshmana: The brother of Sri Rama.

Laxmi, Lakshmi: The Divine Mother as Goddess of Wealth and consort of Vishnu.

Lila: The divine play in which the same actor, God, enacts all the roles.

Lalate: On the forehead. It is believed that the destiny is written on the forehead.

Mahabharata: India's great epic poem that includes the Bhagavad Gita.

Mahabhav: Oneness with the Supreme in the ecstatic sense.

Mahatma: The great One. A holy person. A person who lives for the happiness of others.

Mahamaya: The great Enchantress; the Mother of the Universe; the Divine Reality. Mahamaya is the potency of Brahman; in one aspect She casts a veil over the eyes of creatures to perpetuate the creation; in another aspect She liberates them from the snares of the world.

Mahapurusha: A yogi of very high attainment.

Mahasamadhi: The final passing away of the enlightened ones; a master's conscious leaving of the body to be eternally united with the Cosmic Self.

Mahavir: A name of Hanuman, the monkey devotee of Rama, and prophet of Jains.

Manikarnika Ghat: The famous cremation site at the bank of Ganges at Varanasi. It is believed that Lord Shiva Himself whispers the Divine Mantra into the ears of the dead bodies that are brought to this place for cremation, granting them liberation.

Mantra: The particular name of God, corresponding to the Chosen Ideal of the disciple, with which the disciple is initiated into spiritual life by his Guru. The mantra represents the essence of the Guru's instruction to his disciple who is enjoined to keep it sacred and secret, and to meditate on the aspect of God which it symbolizes for the rest of his life. A mantra is used in japa.

Manosarovar: A grand lake at the foot of the Kailash mountains in the Himalayas.

Maya: Lit., "Illusion". A term of Hindu philosophy denoting ignorance obscuring the vision of reality; the cosmic illusion on account of which the One appears as the many, the Absolute as the relative.

Mohammed: According to Islam, the last of the Divine Messengers sent by Allah, God.

Nishkama Karma: Dedicated action; disinterested action; desireless action.

Nirvikalpa Samadhi: The highest state of Samadhi, the state of formless union with God.

Naisthic Brahmacharin: Unlike Brahmacharin who wear white clothes, Naisthic put on ochre colored robes and are supposed to follow more orthodox rules of celibacy, food, etc., in this order of monkhood.

Om, Aum: The sacred monosyllable is the oldest and most venerated of all Hindu mantras. The 'Om' sound symbolizes the Divine. Om in the undifferentiated word, which has produced all manifestation. The sound form of the Formless.

Paduka: Wooden sandals usually worn by the Sannyasins and Monks. The disciples and devotees worship the Sandals as the embodiment of Guru's Grace.

Paramatman : The Whole. The Ultimate Godhead. The God.

Patanjali: The author of the Yoga Sutras and founder of the yoga system, one of the six systems of orthodox Hindu philosophy which deals with control of the mind, meditation, etc.

Pir, peer: A Sufi saint, teacher.

Prahlad: The son of the demon king Hiranyakashipu, mentioned in the Bhagavatam, who remained steadfast in devotion to Vishnu, his chosen ideal, despite repeated torture and attempts on his life devised by his evil father.

Pranayama: Control of the vital energy (prana) through the practice of breathing exercises.

Prarabdha: Prarabdha is that portion of the accumulated past with which humans are born that determines the happiness and miseries they will experience and through which the soul will develop. The destined, unalterable course which can only be reduced in intensity by Satguru's and God's Grace.

Prasad: Food or any other gift that has been ceremonially offered to God or to a saint. Once blessed, it is usually given to devotees.

Puja: Hindu ritual worship. Puja is designed to concentrate the mind on God and thus to higher devotion.

Pundit: A scholar learned in the Hindu scriptures.

Purana: Ancient mythological narratives linked to the sacred tradition.

Purnavatar: The fullness of God.

Rama: One of the most popular Divine Incarnations of Lord Vishnu and warrior hero of the Ramayana.

Ramakrishna: 1836-1886 A.D. A Godman of unique spiritual capacity, whose life inspired the modern renaissance of Vedanta.

Ramayana: The most ancient Sanskrit epic poem, written by the sage Valmiki, which describes the life of Sri Rama.

Reincarnation: The succession of birth, death and rebirth which results from man's ignorance of his divinity.

Rishi: A seer of Truth to whom the wisdom of the Vedas was revealed.

Sacred thread ceremony: A ritual for a boy born in a Brahmin family. In the presence of the Sacred Fire the boy is initiated in Gayatri mahamantra by a senior Brahmin.

Sadhana: The practice of spiritual disciplines.

Sadhu: True lover of God. The wandering mendicant. The renounced one; a monk; holy man.

Sama Darshana: Refers to the state or the person who beholds the Self in everything. The Bhagavad Gita celebrates such a person as the foremost of yogins.

Samadhi: The super conscious state in which man experiences his identity with the Ultimate Realty. Ecstatic union with God.

Samskara: An impression or tendency created in the mind of a person as the result of an action or thought. The sum total of a person's samskaras including those from previous births forms his character.

Sandhya: The "junction of time" at sunrise midday or sunset. During these times the energy field of Mother Nature is at its highest. Seekers are expected to meditate during these times to get the maximum benefit of external and internal nature.

Sannyasin: A monk who has taken a vow of sannyas renunciation.

Sanskrit: The ancient language of India. Most Hindu scriptures are written in this language.

Sat-Chit-Ananda: Absolute Existence, Absolute Knowledge, Absolute Bliss; aspects of the Brahman.

Satya Yuga: Golden Age.

Shankaracharya: 688-720 A.D. One of the greatest saints and philosophers of India and the foremost exponent of Advaita Vedanta.

Shakti, Sakti: God as mother of the Universe; personification of the primal energy or power of Brahman.

Shiva: Lit., "the Good One." God in His aspect as destroyer of the universe. He is the third person in the Hindu trinity and also worshipped as the Supreme Reality.

Shraddha: Faith in the Truths of the scriptures and in the teachings of the Guru.

Siddhis: Powers that are attained through long and intense spiritual discipline. Sita: Consort of Sri Rama. Daughter of King Janaka.

Sanatana Dharma: The eternal Religion of man based on Timeless principles of Vedas; Traditional name given to Hinduism.

Sitala Devi: A demigoddess who is the harbinger of small-pox.

Sri: The word (which means "revered or "holy") is used as a prefix to honor a deity, a holy personality, or a holy book.

Swarupa: The essential nature of a thing; for example, solidity is a characteristic property of the earth element.

Sufi: One who practices Islamic mysticism.

Sumeru: The sacred Mount Meru of Hindu mythology, Lord Krishna says in Bhagavad Gita that of all the Mountains He is Sumeru. This Mountain situated in the deep North of the Globe is visited by all the celestial beings.

Tantra: A religious philosophy according to which Shakti is usually the main deity worshipped and the universe is regarded as the divine play of Shakti and Shiva.

Upanishads: The sacred Hindu scriptures that contain the philosophical aspect of the Vedas and deal mainly with the knowledge of God and records of the spiritual experiences of the sages of ancient India.

Veda: The most ancient scriptures of the Hindus, regarded by the orthodox as direct divine revelation and supreme authority in all religious matters.

Vedanta: Lit., "the conclusion or essence of the Vedas." A system of philosophy discussed in the Upanishads, the Brahma Sutras, and the Bhagavad Gita.

Vedantin: Vedantin is one who follows the path of Vedantic philosophy of Monism. The Non-dual Self.

Vichara: Discriminating right from wrong, transient from permanent; a state of awareness.

Vital Prana: The vital energy of the body.

Yajna: Ancient Vedic fire ritual.

Yoga: The union of the individual soul with the Supreme Soul. Also, the discipline by which such union is affected.

Yoga Siddha: Yogic perfection.

Yoga Sutras: The famous aphorisms on yoga philosophy and practice, compiled by Patanjali.

Yudisthira: The eldest among the Five Pandava brothers of the great epic of Mahabharata. He is also called as Dharma Raj, the Righteous King.

ABOUT THE AUTHOR

SHUDDHAANANDAA BRAHMACHARI is a globally acclaimed motivational and inspirational speaker, author, spiritual teacher, social advocate and peacemaker. Founder of Stress Management Academy, his Simple Art of Managing Stress and Course in Mindfulness Programs are known worldwide, inspiring corporate leadership, students and spiritual seekers alike.

He is recognized as a visionary social advocate for his development of groundbreaking programs that serve thousands of poverty-stricken individuals in slums of Calcutta, India and remote villages of West Bengal. He founded Lokenath Divine Life Mission in 1985.

His self-authored books include: Your Mind Your Best Friend, Cleaning the Mirror of Mind, Little Book of Meditation, The Heart of Meditation Practice, and The Incredible Life of a Himalayan Yogi.

He was awarded the Man of Peace Award by the World Organization for Peace in 2012 in Mexico. He has spoken at the Parliament of World Religions, United Nations Global Youth Conference and International Conference of Spiritualizing Leadership. He received a Lifetime Achievement Award from the S.T.A.R foundation at the House of Lords in the United Kingdom on July 21, 2015 for his invaluable and outstanding contribution to society.

www.courseinmindfulness.com

https://www.facebook.com/srisri.shuddhaanandaa

https://www.facebook.com/BabaLokenathji

22277108R00161

Printed in Great Britain
by Amazon